BIPOLAR DISORDER

The Truth About Bipolar Disorder and How to Understand and Find the Best Ways to Gain Control

(Understanding the Effects of Bipolar Disorder in The Body and Its Remedies)

Russell F Babcock

Published By Regina Loviusher

Russell F Babcock

All Rights Reserved

Bipolar Disorder: The Truth About Bipolar Disorder and How to Understand and Find the Best Ways to Gain Control (Understanding the Effects of Bipolar Disorder in The Body and Its Remedies)

ISBN 978-1-77485-353-5

Legal & Disclaimer

The information contained in this book is not designed to replace or take the place of any form of medicine or professional medical advice. The information in this book has been provided for educational and entertainment purposes only.

The information contained in this book has been compiled from sources deemed reliable, and it is accurate to the best of the Author's knowledge; however, the Author cannot guarantee its accuracy and validity and cannot be held liable for any errors or omissions. Changes are periodically made to this book. You must consult your doctor or get professional medical advice before using any of the suggested remedies, techniques, or information in this book.

TABLE OF CONTENTS

Introduction

Psychological disorders sufferers are often ignored by the general public. One of the disorders that sufferers face are Bipolar disorder, which is also known as Manic-Depression.

Patients with bipolar disorder typically experience severe mood swings and disturbances that result in them switching between extreme happiness or mania and depressive episodes, at times even to suicidal episodes. Patients suffering from this disorder might appear crazy in the eyes of "normal" people due to their behavior varies according to their mood.

Around 10 million Americans could be classified as bipolar. Around 2.4 percentage of world's population suffers from the condition, according to experts. Bipolar disorder isn't a condition that is congenital however, it usually develops when people are between the ages of 15 to 25 years old.

In contrast to many psychiatric disorders the chances are higher of tackling and managing manic depression with the use of psychotherapy and medications. With the assistance of their family and friends bipolar patients are able to live their lives normally and reduce their mood swings.

This book is designed to assist those suffering from bipolar disorder to understand their condition more clearly and to disprove the belief that they are unresolved cases. It is important to inform anyone that manic depression can be treated and treatment as well as recovery and management of this condition can be completed.

The book is divided into six sections, each of which focus on various features of Bipolar disorder, including its signs and symptoms as well as the main reasons. The other chapter is designed to help define the truth from fiction in relation to this disorder, and another chapter will examine the various psychotherapy methods and medication that are often used to make manic depression episodes less difficult to manage.

Disclaimer The book is primarily meant for self-help purposes and informational purposes only. It is not intended to substitute medical or expert guidance on bipolar disorder. If you believe you or your loved ones suffer from this disorder, don't restrict your knowledge to the information contained in this book.

It is recommended to speak with psychiatrists for an immediate and primary treatment of bipolar disorder. This book can be an additional reference to aid you and your family members cope with bipolar disorder.

Chapter 1: What's Bipolar Disorder in a Scientific Perspective?

Bipolar disorders is an condition of mood regulation, which affects more than 6 million Americans in the present and is due to numerous reasons. It is among the most complicated of all mental disorders. It is a complex condition that has causes of the disorder.

Brain circuit break-up The brain is composed of many cells that form circuits that perform a specific job. These circuits are known as the mood thermostats that regulate the human body. If these circuits fail, there can be a variety of moods like depression, hypomania and mania and the various emotions that accompany them.

Causes of the biological nature - Neurotransmitters are the chemical substances that allow brain cells communicate with one another. When their levels change, this causes bipolar illness. Dopamine can be described as a neurotransmitter that influences depression and hypo mania. Thus, medications that affect dopamine levels are beneficial in combating depression. GABA is the most important inhibitory neurotransmitter. It helps to relax brain cells. Sedative and anti epileptic medications both impact GABA systems. Glutamate is the primary excitatory neurotransmitter found in the brain. If Glutamate levels are excessively high, the brain cell and circuits may be damaged. The lithium and the sodium Valporeate are widely used mood stabilizers that manage the level of GABA and Glutamate.

Intracellular Dysfunction: The brain cells are made up of internal structures known as organelles. Organelles generate energy, interpret genetic codes, and are responsible for protein synthesizing. When the organelles are damaged for any reason, they can cause bipolar disorder.

Human Genetics Scientists have discovered that bipolar disorder could be genetic , or passed down from generation to generation. A variety of genetic combinations could be affected, which can lead to different forms that suffer from bipolar disorders. If identical twins are present when one is diagnosed with bipolar disorder, there's 70% likelihood for the other one to suffer from it.

Environmental Epigenetics - Genes aren't the only factor that determines our identity. The environment we live can also influence our character. The brain's development is influenced by the strain it has experienced throughout the time of our childhood. The environmental influences determine our ability to adapt to different situations. 30percent of the bipolar occurrence is due to epigenetic or environmental causes.

Stress - Brain body circuits such as the HPA (hypothalamopituitary) axis are responsible for the secretion of hormones like adrenaline and cortisol. Stress causes more release of these hormones which can cause mental issues like bipolar disorder, as well as physical ailments like stroke, heart attack as well as cancer. The right amount of testosterone is necessary to bring us into fight or run mode, however excessive levels can cause mental issues.

Oxidative stress Mitochondria transform nutrition of all kinds into chemical energy that is utilized by the brain cells to perform various functions. When bipolar, mitochondria are impacted by stress, and are not capable of producing energy.is which in turn impacts the other bodily functions.

Inflammation - Inflammation that causes illnesses known as cytokines are significantly more prevalent in bipolar patients. They alter the chemical balance in the brain and hinder serotonin. This is why antidepressants fail for bipolar patients. This inflammation is the main reason for the intense outbursts anger, impulsivity, and hostility among bipolar people.

Chapter 2: Signs

Bipolar disorder sufferers often suffer from mood episodes, which are a type of symptom. These are the times when various emotional states occur. These emotional states are typically extreme or intense.

Bipolar disorder can last for a lifetime and the episodes usually disappear, only to occur after a lengthy or short time.

People who are between episodes might be symptom-free and others could experience chronic and persistent symptoms.

There are four distinct kinds of episodes that can be seen for those with bipolar disorder. These include hypomania, manic and depression episodes and hypomania. In the most severe instances the episodes may occur nearly

at the same time, and is referred to as an unmixed state.

What is a depressive episode?

A depressive episode is a mental disorder, which is usually exemplified by a persistent and frequent sadness or low mood. The low mood usually

It is accompanied by a decrease in self-confidence and confidence, and with it a decrease in enthusiasm for one's most satisfying activities. The bipolar disorder of depression is similar to clinical depression.

The symptoms of a depressive episode:

A prolonged period of feeling extremely sad or depressed.

You're no anymore interested in your favorite activities.

*Poor concentration

Inability to make choices.

*Repeated suicidal thoughts or attempts to commit suicide.

*Repeated restlessness and irritation

Sudden changes in sleeping routines, food habits and many other habits.

*Tiredness

* Suicidal thoughts

The signs of a depressive episode in children:

*Explore a small amount of energy and show very little or any interest in activities that are fun.

*Shows a markedly reduced or increased appetite

*Loungs for too long or often

*Doesn't sleep enough

Frequent headaches, or stomach pains

*Repeated feelings of guilt

What is an Manic Episode?

A manic episode is the complete different from a depressive one The mood can fluctuate.

The duration of manic episodes is usually an average of one week. They are characterised by a high, prolonged anger or atypical determination to achieve targets.

Signs of a Manic Episode:

*Intensely happy or cheerful moods.

*Hassy, provocative, or aggressive or aggressive behavior

*Repeated disturbances and restlessness

*Continued involvement in high risk and impulsive behavior

*Impracticable confidence in your own abilities

*Unreasonably committing to a lot of projects, work or obligations

Distracted and easily distracted

*Thoughts on racing

Often changing from one idea to the next

* Talking in a hurried manner

Signs and symptoms of symptoms of Manic episode in children:

*Needs help to focus or remain focused

Talks or thinks about sexually explicit items often

It is possible to experience sleep problems, but isn't tired

*Participates in dangerous actions

*Has a very quick temper.

Extraordinary, yet unusual sensations of happiness

Unusual silliness and funny acts

What exactly is Hypomania?

Hypomania is a milder form of mania.

In a state of hypomanic, there can be feelings of excitement and energy.

However, carrying on doing day-to-day tasks isn't an issue. Hypomanic patients are not a problem.

Many times, they make decisions that damage their careers and their relationships, reputations and their finances.

Signs and symptoms of the Hypomanic State:

*No remorse or concern about the consequences or the consequences

*Impulsiveness, or terrible decision making

Distracted and easily distracted

*Inability to focus

Atypically, optimism or a confidence in one's abilities.

Rapid change of mind

Experience hallucinations or severe delusions.

What is an Mixed State?

Mixed state generally an event that is mixed between depression and the mania.

Mixed states can be present for an extended period of time or may occur in a relatively short period of time.

For instance, in an emotional state, one could feel extremely depressed or helpless yet feel full of energy.

Signs of a Mixed State:

* Assuming an unreal quantity of work, projects or responsibility

*Restlessness and fatigue

*Extreme guilt

*Intense paranoia

Distracted and easily distracted

*Racing thoughts

Often changing from one idea to the next

* Talking in a hurried manner

"Repeatedly thinking about the death of a loved one."

The signs of a mixed state in children:

*Repeated feelings of guilt

It is possible to experience sleep problems, but you're not exhausted

*Has a very quick temper.

* Talks or thinks about sexually explicit items often

Lacks the ability to concentrate or stay focused

Distracted and easily distracted

*Explore a small amount of energy and show minimal or any interest in activities that are fun.

*Poor concentration

These are just a few of the most prominent indicators and symptoms that those who suffer from bipolar disorder typically display.

If these symptoms become too intense, they can easily turn psychotic or exaggerated. For instance, if your depression is excessive, you could be tempted to believe that you've done something incredibly wrong like killing someone or committed a crime or very poor. Those experiencing intense maniac episodes my

Feel like you're a famous, wealthy or famous person, or even an awe-inspiring superhero or possess supernatural powers.

Chapter 3: Conventional Medicine for Bipolar Disorder

The medication regimen is the basis of treatment for bipolar disorder. Treatment can bring your anxiety and depression in check, and stop relapses once your mood stabilizes.

Tips to get the most value from medications for bipolar disorder

Beware of antidepressants. The treatment you receive for bipolar depression is different from normal depression treatment. Instead of stopping it, antidepressants may cause bipolar disorder to worsen or trigger manic episodes. Begin with mood stabilizers, and avoid taking antidepressants if you are not on them.

Keep taking medication: Continue taking medications, even if you are feeling better. If you stop abruptly using your bipolar medication your chances of relapse are extremely high. Talk to your doctor prior to making any changes, even if you believe you don't require medication anymore.

Incorporate therapy into therapy as part of your plan for treatment: Research has shown that taking medication in combination with therapy can aids patients suffering from bipolar disorder more effectively than taking just prescribed medication. Therapy will track your progress, aids in overcome life's challenges and aid in dealing with issues that bipolar disorder can be making your life difficult.

Natural mood stabilisers: The way you live your life can have a significant influence on bipolar disorder symptoms. We'll discuss this further in the future.

Here are a few medications to help treat bipolar disorder.

Lithium is a mood stabilizer

Mood stabilizers are the foundation of treatment for bipolar disorder in both depression and manic episodes. Lithium is a most trusted and well-known mood stabilizers and extremely effective for treating bipolar depression and mania. But, it's not effective against fast-cycling varieties or mixed types of bipolar disorder.

Anticonvulsant - mood stabilizers

Anticonvulsants originally were developed for treatments for epilepsy however they are also able to alleviate the symptoms of mania as well as reduce the severity of mood swings. They can be used to treat:

Depakote also known as Valproic acid. The drug is an extremely efficient mood stabilizer. The most popular brand name is Depakene or Depakote. Valproic acid is often the first option for mixed mania such as rapid cycling or mania that causes hallucinations or delusions.

Other medications to treat bipolar disorder include

Topiramate (Topamax)

Lamotrigine (Lamictal)

Carbamazepine (Tegretol)

Antidepressant drugs

It is important to take antidepressants in moderation as they aren't effective for people suffering from bipolar depression. A number of studies have demonstrated that they are ineffective or perform no better than placebo. Antidepressants can cause manic episodes in those with bipolar disorder. If you take an antidepressant with no mood stabilizer is often the cause of the onset of a manic episode. Additionally, antidepressants can trigger mood-cycling.

Mood stabilizers

Below are some mood-stabilizers to assist

Symbyax

Zyprexa (olanzapine)

Seroquel (quetiapine)

Lamictal (lamotrigine)

Antipsychotic medication for bipolar disorder

Your physician may prescribe an antipsychotic drug in the event that you are unable to connect with reality during a depressive or manic episode. If mood stabilizers don't prove efficient, then antipsychotic drugs might be a good option. The majority of antipsychotic medicines are combined along with mood stabilizers to get more effective results. Here are some medications that are antipsychotic:

Risperidone (Risperdal)

Quetiapine (Seroquel)

Ziprasidone (Geodon)

Clozapine (Clozaril)

Ariprazole (Abilify)

Olanzapine (Zyprexa)

Other medicines for bipolar disorder

Benzodiazepines. They are fast-acting and produce a sedative effects in 30 minutes to one hour. The majority of mood stabilisers require some time to ease bipolar symptoms. The doctor can prescribe benzodiazepines for symptoms of agitation or insomnia, or anxiety.

Calcium channel blockers The calcium channel blockers were created to combat hypertension and coronary problems However, they also provide an effect on mood stability. In comparison to conventional mood stabilizers, these are less effective, however they are less likely to cause negative side negative effects.

Thyroid medications: Bipolar disorder patients often suffer from an imbalance of thyroid hormone within their bodies. Thyroid medication is a highly effective bipolar depression treatment that has only few adverse consequences.

Chapter 4: The Causes, Symptoms, and Types of Bipolar Disorder

It's common for all human beings to experience mood swings at times What can you do to determine whether you may have bipolar disorder? The answer is in the fact that you experience instances that are referred to by the term "mood instances." They generally involve periods of intense emotional states, however it's possible for someone to feel more than one emotion at the same moment. Patients who experience multiple of them in a single day or who are prone to lingering in one mood for prolonged periods of time are likely to be suffering from bipolar disorder. Be aware that it's recommended to consult a certified medical professional to evaluate the patient to determine if there is a possibility of experiencing bipolar disorders.

Perhaps, the most obvious indication of the severity of a patient's situation could be is how often they change between the mood states:

1.) Depressive episodes. In the moments when a patient is suffering from such a mood-related episode they will experience an overwhelming sense of despair and despair. In the end, the patient could exhibit little or any interest in the things which once brought them satisfaction, and could even begin to avoid engaging with family members without explanation. Patients can also display drastic shifts in eating habits or sleeping routines (i.e. sleeping in a large amount or none at all) as well as consider suicide during the time.

A bipolar patient is required to be placed on a suicide monitor if they start to display the following types of behavior:

A lot of times, we withdraw from contact with outside and especially family members

Making arrangements for the personal matters of their clients (e.g. writing wills, distributing precious possessions, etc.)

Discussion of the idea of suicide

2.) Manic episodes. In stark contrast to depression-related episodes Manic episodes are defined by an increase in energy levels and activity in patients. Although these episodes are typically classified to an individual's "highs," not all manic episodes are characterized by emotions of joy or feelings of euphoria. Someone who exhibits excessive anxiety or restlessness is equally likely to have the symptoms of a manic episode like someone who appears to be in a state of bliss. The most prominent symptoms for patients experiencing an episode of manic depression are short attention spans as well as quick speech movements.

Since manic episodes may cause patients to be more active than they normally are (and consequently become more productive) People often believe that they're nothing more than beneficial on the part of the patient. However, the heightened energy and fragmented attention spans that are common in manic episodes could cause the patient to engage in reckless actions (e.g. sexual sex that is not protected and gambling too much, etc.)

In addition to experiencing the two mood swings mentioned in the previous paragraph, bipolar sufferers can be in a mixed state , where they suffer from both manic and depression symptoms. For instance, a person may appear to be functionally high and depressive at simultaneously. In all types menopausal episodes major modifications to the patients' sleep and eating habits are evident.

The nature of the majority (if but not always) mental problems is the fact that they're extremely complex, and there's more than one cause for them. The three main causes of the majority of bipolar disorders are:

1.) Environmental factors. These are among the most frequent and the most potent triggers. Any event in life that creates an increased level of trauma stress on an individual can cause them to develop predispositions to bipolar disorder that are not apparent. A loss of someone close to you or a long-term illness or even a very demanding job could contribute to the development of a bipolar disorder.

2.) Genetic influences. As with many types of mental disorders, bipolar disorder may be much more prevalent in certain families than other. So, a person who has at least two relatives (such like a parent or an older sibling) with the disorder may be more susceptible to suffer from the illness than people who have no relatives who are afflicted by the disorder.

3.) biological factors. Human moods and feelings are affected by the activity of their brains and how certain neurotransmitters function. Dopamine and serotonin are two hormones are the main reason for feelings of happiness and general wellbeing have been proven to be ineffective in the majority of people suffering from bipolar disorder.

If a patient is identified as having bipolar disorders the following step will be to identify the kind they are suffering from. This will ensure that the therapist is able to prescribe the appropriate treatment.

There are around five kinds that are bipolar:

1.) Bipolar I. This is a classic example that shows bipolar disorders. Patients with Type 1 Bipolar Disorder exhibit extreme mood swings and are often found spending varying amounts durations in either depressive or manic state.

2.) Bipolar II. This kind of bipolar disorder is frequently misinterpreted as depression because patients experience more manic episodes than depressive ones.

3.) Mixed Episodes. Patients suffering from this type of bipolar disorder exhibit symptoms of manic as well as depression episodes. They may therefore engage in risky activities that require high energy levels yet feel depressed and depressed.

4.) Rapid-cycling. Rapid-cycling is when you experience at the very least four depressive or manic (or both) instances in a year.

5.) Cyclothymia. It is generally referred to as a milder version of the bipolar disorder, it is typically characterized by hypomanic (a lesser heightened manic mood in which a person appears to be less cheerful or active than they normally are) and depression-related episodes. But, this type in bipolar disorders is recognized as a chronic disorder, one that may last up to two years.

Chapter 5: The Lifestyle Changes

As we have mentioned the need for lifestyle changes is crucial to manage symptoms that are associated with bipolar disorder. These tips for living a healthy lifestyle help make bipolar disorder manageable

Escape Stress Stress

Stress is the primary cause of both manic and depression episodes. If you wish to avoid or reduce these episodes, you need be able to manage stress. Here are a few actions you can take to ease stress and increase relaxation

Maintain your personal and work space tidy and clutter-free. If you are suffering from bipolar disorder, there is plenty of mental clutter. To avoid having sexually explicit thoughts, it can aid in keeping your personal and professional space tidy and organized. Make sure you label all drawers. It is easier to locate things. Set a routine to sweep your floors every week at least and make sure your belongings are organised. It is also recommended to vacuum your floor and eliminate all dirt at the least two times each week.

Enjoy upbeat or relaxing music. Like we said earlier music can have a relaxing effect , so if you're feeling low wear a headset and enjoy positive music. You can also dance to songs and motivational music. If you're tired it's a good idea to play calm and slow music. This can help to calm and ease your tension. If you're feeling under the stress, take a breather and listen to some soothing music.

Note down all your worries, and then worry about just one thing at a. This will make you relax.

Start a journal or an online blog. Journaling about your experience concerns, worries, and challenges can help you manage your mood.

Avoid the negative people that are in your life. They are the ones who are critical of your character and make you feel bad about yourself. They are determined to make you feel down and will do whatever it takes in order to cause you miserable. They will also try to gain advantage over your vulnerability, so avoid them.

Relax and take a break. Stress and anxiety can worsen the symptoms of depression in those suffering from bipolar disorder. Therefore, it's important to find a way to unwind. After work, you can sit down and watch your preferred TV program. You could also hang out with some with your pals or visit the spa to receive an oil massage.

Don't take your life or yourself too seriously. For better control of your symptoms. It is important to avoid taking your life too seriously. Learn to laugh at work. You can also enjoy funny movies and TV shows. You can also view humorous clips on YouTube also.

Take note of at least one good event that occurred today. Every day, you should take the time to consider at least one positive moment that took place throughout the day. It will make you help you to realize that the day was not all bad and that your life isn't as bad.

Give hugs to the people you cherish. Hugging people you cherish is extremely relaxing. You can also hug your pets too.

Pause for a moment. If everything seems overwhelming Take a step back, and take time out. This will allow you to clear your mind and help prevent possibility of a depression or manic episodes.

Exercise

Exercise can help stabilize your mood. It assists in balancing and controlling the neurotransmitters that are present in your brain. Actually, it increases creation of serotonin endorphins, serotonin, and other neurotransmitters and hormones which have a mood-stabilizing impact. Additionally, exercise can help you control your weight and keep your body in shape and healthy. You can perform a wide range of exercises, such as:

Running

Running is an amazing exercise. It increases your endurance, and can help to shed weight. Running is also an excellent means of releasing serotonin and endorphins. To control your bipolar disorder, run or jog for at minimum 30 minutes every day. However, you must be cautious when doing this particularly if you're experiencing a manic episode. Limit your physical activity to maximum, 2 minutes per day. Exercise or physical activity that is excessive is a sign of mania therefore be cautious.

Cycling

You can cycle around your neighborhood each morning. The exercise can increase the heart rate. This can help you burn calories, and also help you manage your symptoms.

Yoga

Yoga is a fantastic exercise that offers a variety of positive effects on your mental health. It enhances your cognitive functioning and helps you improve your mood as well. It assists patients with bipolar disorders to get and remain connected to their body and thoughts. It helps patients become conscious of their mood changes.

Yoga can help decrease depression, anxiety as well as neurotic symptoms and anger. Here are a few yoga postures that can alleviate signs of bipolar disorder.

1. Utthita Marichyasana, or standing Sage Marichi Pose

This posture is stimulating the part of your body known as the cerebellum. This will help you manage your emotions.

2. From Hand to Leg Pose as well Padahastasana

This pose increases blood flow to the brain. It also improves cognitive performance and also can help you control your mood as well.

3. Bhumi Pada Mastakasana or "Feet, Hand, and Head on Earth" Pose

This is an exercise that is deep forward bend. This pose can also increase the circulation of blood into the brain. The pose can be challenging, so it is best practice it under the guidance by a yoga instructor.

Yoga can help you manage your mood. It also can help you live your life in many different ways. It helps you remain grounded. It assists you in focusing on the present. It also reduces hallucinations, delusions and other symptoms.

Apart from running, yoga as well as biking, you could also try many other workouts. Try dancing and swimming. However, you must exercise at a moderate pace.

Establish A Strong Support Group

If you're struggling with bipolar disorder, it's crucial to form a group of support.

Keep in mind that psychotherapy and medications are only effective for a certain amount of time. Therefore, it is important to get help from those close to you. It is important to talk to those you can trust. Share your troubles and worries. Ask for compassion from the people who are around you. Being a bipolar patient isn't an easy task however, it is manageable, particularly if you surround yourself with supportive and compassionate people.

Join bipolar support groups. You are also able to join civic clubs. These clubs can keep you entertained during depression episodes, and keep you grounded when you are experiencing manic episodes.

It is a good idea to connect with the person you love every day at least once. Take as many outings as you can, and try to stay away from social loneliness.

Get enough sleep

Sleep is crucial for those who suffer from bipolar disorder. In order to control your mood, you need at least eight hours of rest each day. It is also crucial to set a regular time for sleeping. This means that you must to get up and sleep at the same time every day.

Do not put a lot of Things on Your To-Do List

When you're suffering from manic episodes You'll feel as though you're able to do anything, so it's best not to adding a number of things to onto your agenda. This will reduce anxiety and stress.

Make Sure You Take Care of Yourself

Bipolar patients often stay in their homes for months. They are not eating well and often don't even get baths. To manage those bipolar disorders, you need to look after your self. It is essential to maintain a healthy lifestyle and ensure that you get a bath each day. Make sure you visit your friends frequently as it will provide you with an incredibly strong sense of belonging. Find something you enjoy doing every day. You could write or you can draw. Find ways to be creative in how you convey your thoughts and feelings.

Practice Gratitude

If you're suffering from the bipolar disorder, you'll feel that you're not the luckiest person on earth. You'll feel as though you're dealing with all the issues that life has to offer. If this happens, you should take a look at the bright side, and begin taking note of your blessings.

Thank God that you're alive. Bipolar disorder is not an easy task, however, there's still plenty of reasons to be grateful about.

Be thankful for all the people in your life and especially those who cherish and encourage you.

Be grateful for the material possessions you are currently enjoying. If you have an apartment to sleep in as well as a car and an occupation You are a fortunate person. So, be thankful.

Even if you're suffering from bipolar disorder, you're nonetheless more fortunate than you imagine. Be thankful.

Keep in Touch with the Real World

As we have discussed in the previous guide, mindfulness is crucial because it helps keep people connected to reality. The most crucial aspect of mindfulness is for those suffering with bipolar disorder.

If you are suffering from bipolar disorder, you need to keep a steady mind in all you do.

When you type take note of the way your fingers are hitting every key on the keyboard.

Food critics should eat like food. Be attentive to the appearance of your food. Also, take the time to note the distinct tastes in your meal.

Pay attention to your thoughts. Take note of your thoughts. Which are the self-defeating beliefs? What are your ill-conceived notions of the grandeur of your life? Do you believe that you are not worthy of the love and happiness you deserve? Do you believe you're destined to help save the world? Here are a few affirmations to keep you on track:

I deserve love.

I am deserving.

I am a valuable person.

I'm worthy and valuable however, I don't believe that I am special.

I'm sure that I'm similar to other people.

I don't possess any superpowers. I'm intelligent however, my intelligence is not superpower.

I accept responsibility to my choices.

I must be careful not to engage in irresponsible behaviour.

I'll take my time before I make a choice.

To manage both the depressive and manic symptoms, it is important to remain grounded.

Healthy Diet

A healthy diet is vital for those with bipolar disorder. We will go over the subject in depth within the following chapter.

Clean Living

In order to effectively manage your bipolar disorder, you must stay clear of the use of alcohol or illegal substances. All of your efforts will go off the table when you consume alcohol or take illegal substances. You have to be accountable for yourself and stay away from the activities that could cause your mood issues.

Make Note of Your Moods

It is vital to keep track of your mood. This will assist you in managing your symptoms better. Every day, record what you feel in an account in a journal. Be aware of thoughts of suicide. If you are thinking of suicide or death you must seek immediate help.

The battle against bipolar disorder isn't an easy task. However, it is possible to get it achieved. Therefore, you must be active and take the necessary steps to improve your lifestyle. Making changes to your lifestyle can keep you sane and save your life.

Chapter 6: Protect Your Psychology

The equation so far is:

Lifestyle + Natural Products = BPD is overcome

Do you think this is enough? It's not enough. There are additional issues that influence your mental health, which is the most critical factor to beating any illness. These concerns include:

1) Sleep.

One of the signs that are characteristic of the bipolar disorder the lack of sleep when in the manic period. However, since the body has to regulate this, during the time of depression the body is in a state of sleep. If BPD causes the beginning of anxiety, it will turn into a sleep nightmare.

Your body needs sufficient rest every day. If you can't sleep, use sedatives. If you're unable to get up, set a noisy alarm clock that is placed away from your bed to force you to get up in order to turn it off. What's the best amount of rest do for you?

You'll be less agitated

Keep yourself from feeling sick anxious or depressed.

Help you in decision making.

Some other things you can do to ensure that you get sufficient sleep include:

Do not drink alcohol or coffee before going to sleep.

Keep the temperature in your bedroom at a at a comfortable temperature.

Keep your bedroom as dark as possible.

Be sure to exercise at a reasonable time during the day.

Learn about relaxation techniques.

2)Do not stop taking your medication.

A few patients suffering from bipolar disorder who notice that their symptoms have gone discontinue taking their medication. This is a huge error. Always keep using your medication until your doctor who is treating you says that they are not. If you stop taking them before the prescribed time, the chance of rebound is too high. Take them on even if it is difficult to tolerate the adverse effects. Be aware that the majority of them are temporary.

3)Include psychotherapy

The sessions of psychotherapy, and even the those with a partner, are extremely vital. Bipolar disorders is considered to be a psychological disorder. It requires treatment through the human brain. This will allow you to be able to discern what you see and the images you think you are seeing, and know what's going on within your brain.

4)Manage your health at work

The work-related issues are among of the major causes for anxiety, stress BPD and other mental illnesses. Particularly in jobs where is under greater pressure to deliver outcomes, or, when you are the boss, you're putting pressure on you to produce results in order that your company is successful. Here's a list of things you can do in your work hours. If you're an employee the medical note allows you to carry out these tasks whatever your employer tells you:

Make sure you take regular breaks. If you feel your stress levels are rising then take a break prior to the time you feel like you'll blow up in the face of someone or an apathetic incident is coming to your door.

Try to breathe deeply

Walk around the block while listening to a relaxing playlist (not enough to cause you to fall sleep but!)

Make a call to a friend or plan the time to meet with your councilor.

5)DO not give up!

It is easy to understand and its importance can't be overemphasized. It is repeatedly in this article that it is said that you must be determined to improve. It's simple. The moment you quit, you don't want to improve your performance.

With these issues now been resolved you are moving closer to the desired outcome. There are still some issues that need to be taken into consideration.

Chapter 7: Principles Of Cbt

Cognitive Behavioral Therapy (CBT) is typically suggested as a an integral part of the treatment program for bipolar. It helps by altering the mood swings and reducing the extremes. The treatment focuses on linking thoughts and emotions to physical actions , so that you can stop the negative thoughts. This method helps you recognize your negative thoughts similar to positive thinking however instead of changing your mind, you react in a gentler manner. It's an approach that could aid you in overcoming your struggles with positive thinking techniques.

What is the process?

CBT is a type which helps with cognitive restructuring. It helps you alter your mental outlook and fix problems. Therapy is usually a process where you're taught to spot and recognize distortions and exaggerated thinking and realize that they originate from your illness and not reality.

It's a great way to avoid massive changes before they occur. It's a type of problem-solving that lets you be aware of the issue using your mind, then think of solutions, and make a sensible decision without fearing. It is applicable to any area of life when stress is present and could lead to a fall.

What exactly is it?

CBT is a combination of methods that work together to help your everyday life more efficient and stay more steady. The first step in making use of CBT is accepting the diagnosis. A lot of people try to avoid the stigma surrounding mental health issues by not acknowledging that they have them However, it has been established that brain function of sufferers is physically different , which isn't only untrue but also unhelpful. Accepting the diagnosis makes the idea of reaching out and seeking assistance much more attainable. If you're willing to reach out, you'll also be in a position to gain access to a lot of the help that is available around you , such as social groups, religious communities as well as professional assistance. This can also assist you by making you aware of your signs and triggers, so you're better able to prevent these or deal with the symptoms when they arise.

Monitoring

One of the components of CBT is keeping track of your own behavior. Bipolar is a particularly difficult illness to treat since the symptoms can change. On a regular basis you can experience extreme mood swings or be unresponsive for days at a. Be conscious of your thoughts as well as your actions, and recording the details down will help doctors to better recommend methods for the treatment you need. Assessing your mood every day Noting any specific events or changes, or even noting any relaxing actions as well as your response to medication are a an integral part of a comprehensive treatment strategy.

Monitoring yourself implies that you'll come to recognize triggers and indicators so you're able to stay clear of them. Common triggers are typically stress-related, and may include arguments, financial problems with colleagues and students as well as sleep issues, as well as seasonal shifts. Both depression and mania have distinct warning signs when relapses are occurring, so it is important to be aware of these signs so that you can prevent them from happening.

When you're depressed, craving chocolate is one of the most obvious indicators, but there's also an inordinate need to sleeping, a desire to be alone as well as an absence of motivation. Mania is usually defined by having a constant hunger being energized but unable to focus, and becoming angry. Be aware of these signs and monitoring them will help ensure that they aren't lost in the midst of your day and the issue can spiral. If you recognize the patterns before they become apparent, you can take them off your radar. off.

Example Shay:

She's very busy always on the go, but at times she's unable to get up. After being diagnosed, the medication worked but it also led to feel dizzy and make her take days of each month off from feeling sick. In the normal course of her work her boss would be very demanding at weekends, and she would feel stressed. When she received emails from her boss, Shay instantly felt that she might be in danger, and would begin to panic. The more she pondered it, the more she'd be worried and, over the course of the weekend, she would feel depressed. On Fridays, she would find herself craving chocolate and frequently leave early for work with an intense headache. Then she would lie in bed on Saturdays in bed. By observing her symptoms, she could tell the fact that her reactions to emails from her boss were triggers for her depression during the weekend, and she took actions to rectify her thinking.

Another aspect of CBT is the creation of an established routine. A regular schedule is a great way to maintain stability and avoid being affected by stress. A regular schedule allows the proper amount of sleep, meals and chores, and social plans. It also allows for exercises to enjoy the benefits of alternative treatments and medications and still function well. One of the most difficult aspects of bipolar disorder is frequently making excuses during your depression so you don't take action and if you follow a routine, you're less likely to stray and not be productive, which could result in the spiral downward. The routine serves as an alarm to prevent this.

Maximizing Treatment

CBT works only If you're using it in during sessions of therapy. To be able to use it to be successful, you have to develop a regularity, self-monitoring and accept that the diagnosis is correct. Changes in your thought patterns isn't easy, which is why therapy can be helpful however, you must ensure that you repeat the same actions throughout the sessions as well. Your actions must be self-regulating, and they should be able to stop abruptly.

Example: Phil

He's taking his medications as it's his job and is going to therapy, but after a few days, he's relapsed and gets stressed , then quickly slides into depression. His therapist utilizes CBT to stop the trigger which causes him to fall. Phil creates a regular daily routine, and then begins to note the state of mind he's experiencing and the causes changes. The therapist reviews the data with him and suggests making changes to his routine in order to avoid these triggers.

Chapter 8: Ayurveda

Ayurveda is the next approach we'll explore for aiding with bipolar disorder. If you don't already know, Ayurveda is a term which refers to a kind of Hindu traditionalist treatment. The practice places emphasis on the link between physical and mental ideas and is a different method that's effects are connected to helping patients suffering from bipolar disorder improve their well-being. To comprehend the way Ayurveda functions, it's essential to be aware that it's split into two distinct parts. The first is the body that enhances the physical form while the other is the mind or mentality that is particularly important when solving the problems that arise from bipolar disorder.

Bipolar illness is difficult illness, however it is possible to conquered. This concept is the basis of Ayurveda which can bring advantages through "balancing" between the mind and body. It is like the way Acupuncture helps to balance the channels of the body, however instead of needles you employ a variety of methods. Herbs, along with lifestyle and diet changes are just a few examples of the techniques used. Each one of them has positive effects that can improve your health by influencing your mental and physical health.

Ayurveda relies on your body's well-balanced state. This balance is essential to health and the well-being that is derived from Ayurveda is not possible without it. This is the result of an ancient way of thinking that helps you to determine the most effective solution to assist you. With this type of thinking, every person is guided by three distinct principles for mind and body, which are known as Vata, Pitta and Kapha.. These three principles are referred to as "doshas". Every "dosha" is different for everyone, and by through the use of herbs and the changes described below, you can aid in balancing your doshas. This is crucial, as being imbalanced in your doshas can cause a variety of issues. These imbalances result from improper use in the human body like an insufficient amount of exercising.

The basic idea behind Ayurveda is very effective in helping to reduce signs of depression. Since depression is among the most common effects of bipolar disorder, it's simple to understand why using this approach to fight depression is beneficial. But, aside from this benefit, Ayurveda could be beneficial to those who aren't being successful with their prescribed medications. Ayurveda has been proven to have specific effects on our bodies and side effects are commonplace in the modern world. These adverse effects can be especially strong when it comes to the treatment of bipolar disorder. If you're not getting the results you want from traditional medications or treatments that are not working, it might be a good idea consider using herbs and treatments that are associated with Ayurveda. This is because most of the herbs utilized to treat this condition are more well-liked by patients in comparison to traditional medications.

In a research study (Qureshi and colleagues., Neuropsychiatric Disease and Treatment. 2013 9:639) it was discovered that Ayurveda can provide numerous benefits that can help in reducing the symptoms associated with bipolar disorder. The diagnosis is based on an extensive background, thorough physical exam as well as the assessment of vital signs , including pulse and other relevant laboratory tests. But, results from tests related to Ayurveda are not conclusive at times. This is typically because the majority of results are based on one particular person, instead of a wider group. Furthermore, these kinds of plants can be slow in altering or affecting moods however this is the case in the majority of herbal therapies used for treating mood disorders. But, this is different with Ayurveda because the herbs that are used in this treatment are known to have more affects on mood. A few preliminary studies on major depression that were treated with herbs, herbal mixes as well as Rasayanas (a particular section of Ayurveda that aims to re-energize and nourish the body at every level and includes a variety of products made using a mixture with herbs) have shown improvement in depression scores.

Clinical depression is among the most prevalent issues associated in bipolar disorder. Since this disorder isn't always treated effectively with conventional treatments, Ayurveda and the modifications to your lifestyle, along with herbal supplements, could be an extremely effective alternative method of treatment. If you decide to utilize Ayurveda as a means to treat mental illnesses it is important to be aware of the kind of herbs you choose to utilize. Similar to aromatherapy, be aware of the importance of conducting your own research, in along with consulting experts.

This is because certain forms of Ayurveda have been found to contain toxic chemicals or metals in the products. The lacing process can have huge negative effects on your health. Some herbs do not contain harmful substances, however. If you are able to identify the best choices related to Ayurveda and Ayurveda, you'll be in good shape.

Chapter 9: Environment And Self-Help

The management of bipolar disorder is an enormous burden for patients to carry on their own. Most of the time the outcome of treatment is mostly on the level of help and guidance patients receive from their family members and acquaintances. Patients with bipolar disorders cannot be treated on their own particularly if they are susceptible to extreme depressive or manic episodes.

Patients can risk others and themselves when they are in the grip of a particularly frightening episode, accompanied by psychosis and extravagant thoughts. Bipolars with bipolar disorder are known to exhibit suicidal tendencies whereas others tend to engage in dangerous behavior during manic-depressive episodes. Some may even commit crimes during the peak of their symptoms.

Family Guide and friends of Bipolar Patients

No matter if you're a fan whether you like it or not, are involved when someone around you suffers from bipolar disorder. The first step to do is make sure that the patient is recognized immediately by a healthcare professional. This is the first step to treatment, particularly when the patient is experiencing massive manic episodes and would therefore resist treatment.

Instruct the patient to take care of the patient. If you can, be with the patient when he consults with a physician. You could even set up an appointment for family therapy to ensure that everyone involved in the family. If the patient starts to stop taking treatment because it appears that he's getting better It is your responsibility to make sure that the patient is still receiving treatment to ensure that he doesn't experience a relapse.

The first thing your loved one requires are love, patience and understanding. If it is helpful you to find more details about bipolar disorder to ensure you are aware of the right way to handle the patient.

Sometimes, people with bipolar disorders just need someone to be able to listen and accept. They require an environment in which they are able to feel comfortable to share their thoughts and in which there aren't likely triggers that can trigger the onset of a manic depressive episode.

It is also possible to provide your loved ones with activities such as walks, excursions or other leisure activities that will keep him focused on his illness. In the end, you have to be a strong presence that will help your loved one through and remind him of the importance of regular care.

Be alert for any changes in your friend's relatives' moods and health. When you first notice a symptom it is important to inform the physician immediately to ensure that a serious episode is prevented.

Pay attention for the patients thoughts as well as loose remarks, particularly if it is about his self-image and idea of suicide. These thoughts and comments must always be reported to the psychiatrist who is treating him.

Here are some indicators that a bipolar patient may be considering suicide:

The constant discussion of suicide and death. The patient has an euphoric outlook and frequently speaks of death or the possibility of dying early. He's not able to finish his work and he moves mechanicallyand isn't able to clearly look around or at anyone in the vicinity.

A feeling of helplessness and hopelessness. Joy is taken away from the patient. He is not able to find joy in the activities that he once enjoyed. He's always worried about the outcomes of events. He is engulfed in sadness and despair like he's being pulled into a dark emotional hole.

Involvement in extremely risky activities which is similar to having an aspiration to die. The patient is involved in activities they never did before and is often at the possibility of being arrested, injured or even killed. Excessive spending, gambling and even use of drugs as well as social activities that aren't so safe could indicate that the person isn't concerned about placing his life in danger.

The feelings of guilt and insanity. The patient lacks self-esteem to be proud of and constantly apologizes for the wrongs that he's done and that he's not worthy of any love or respect. He is unloved, insecure and unworthy, regardless of what people around him tell him otherwise.

Making arrangements and always saying goodbye to loved ones. He's constantly telling you what to do when he's gone. He's telling you not to cry or grieve for his presence and that you have to move on without the person you love. It's like he's training you to lose him soon.

Are you looking for tools that can be used to commit suicide (e.g. sharp objects, pills rope). The man doesn't just want to take his own life but he's determined to act upon it, looking for an item that could be used to end his life.

If someone is on the verge of to suicide, do not allow him to be left alone, in a place where he could harm himself. Be sure to keep dangerous tools and objects out of his reach, however do not cause him to feel lonely. Keep talking to him as another person is able to call for assistance immediately.

Support Groups

Bipolar disorder is difficult to manage not just for the individual but for all those involved with the issue. Everyone is affected in some way, particularly as a result of the actions of your loved one when they are suffering from an episode of depression or manic. You may even be set back financially (spending on a spree) as well as emotional (major Depression episodes) or any other type of behavior problems that are caused by the disorder.

When dealing with bipolar disorders it's crucial to keep a focus not just on the well-being of the patient, but also on those who are around him. Being a caregiver for bipolar people long-term is a bit exhausting and stressful. It could affect the whole family's health and well-being.

In the present, the most effective option is to go through therapy with your bipolar patient. Stressed caregivers more often than not increases the likelihood that a bipolar patient could be relapsed and have a major manic-depressive episode.

There are many support groups, not just for bipolar patients , but as well for caregivers. These support groups are designed to help the family members and patients learn more about the bipolar disorder. It also lets them connect with other people who have experienced similar situations as well as seek help and generally ease any anxiety that may have developed due to their experiences with bipolar disorder.

Self-Help Guide

If you're suffering from bipolar disorder, then you must be able to manage it rather than having it control you. It's not straightforward, but rehabilitation and treatment are dependent on how you deal with and manage the situation. Sometimes, a change in lifestyle is required to lessen the triggers that can trigger bipolar episodes to happen.

The first thing to do is should increase your knowledge about bipolar disorder when it is confirmed that you suffer from the condition. This will allow you to better know your condition and help you understand the advantages of seeking treatment. It will also assist you to understand your situation and realize the fact that you have hope of finding the cure.

It's essential to get away from stressful situations as stress is usually one of the main factors that trigger bipolar episodes. Try to balance your priorities and to take time to relax with practices and techniques such as yoga and deep breathing.

Don't isolate yourself particularly when you notice the first signs of an illness coming. Be sure to surround yourself with your family and friends and inform them promptly whenever you notice a shift in your mood. If you're not on good relations with your family members Try looking for an online support group within your area, or speak to a trusted friend to release your stress.

Select healthy alternatives instead of pushing yourself beyond the limits. Fighting the bipolar disorder can be a decision made by a person's lifestyle. Better sleeping, better eating and living a healthier lifestyle generally will allow you to get back to health faster, improve your mood, and guarantee that you don't have other significant episodes.

Keep a journal in which you monitor your day-to-day moods, and also look for signs of any type of episode. It's crucial to identify any major symptoms and have it addressed prior to it turning into a full-blown depression or mania.

Do not miss your medication until you know the best dosage for you. Always consult your physician prior to making any decision regarding the dosage or the discontinuation or discontinuation of the medication. Bipolar disorder typically requires a maintenance medication to keep your mood under control.

Don't depend on self-help to treat bipolar disorder, even if your symptoms appear like they aren't necessarily alarming. It is important to seek advice from an expert in all forms of psychological disorders , including this one, particularly in the area of medication and treatment.

If you're thinking about self-harming or suicide You must seek assistance immediately.

Chapter 10: Signs and symptoms of recognizing Borderline Personality Disorder

It is crucial to be able to detect the symptoms for borderline disorder, so that the person struggling with it be it you or another person, is capable of getting the assistance they require as fast as they can. It can be difficult to tell if someone is suffering from the disorder because they often tend to avoid others. The people around them will believe that their mood swings are the result of a long and tiring day. they'll often assume that the person is surrounded by relatives and friends in other aspects of their lives, rather than being by themselves.

Being aware of some of the signs of personality disorders can assist in helping the sufferer when they require help. We'll go into greater specifics about the particulars of these symptoms and signs However, the general idea is that the most common symptoms you will notice when dealing with people suffering from borderline personality disorder are:

A variety of mental health problems like anger, substance abuse as well as anxiety, anger and depression. When they suffer from Borderline Personality Disorder, the underlying causes may cause things to get more difficult and, if they don't start treatment for the depression, anger or another issue the sufferer is not likely to be able to being better.

They just want an adrenaline rush out of their lives. So they'll engage in something that is enjoyable and involves a great deal of risk. This is a method for them to gain a bit of release from their emotions that they can't be in control for just an hour or so. However, the problem is when the excitement has ended. It is likely that they will start feeling as if they did something wrong , and the anxiety and guilt will be more intense than at the start. This could turn into an endless spiral of trying hard to get better but with no outcomes.

Self-harming behavior - this could include actions like burning or cutting their own bodies, or even the use of drugs. This will occur because the person suffering from this disorder will keep all of their feelings in their own head. They seldom, if ever, be hurtful to other people when they are angry or angry, but instead will hurt themselves. They might also do it due to the fact that they don't think that they're worth something and thus

People with this type of personality disorder are constantly worried about being left behind. Most of the time, this is their own fault they may be angry at people trying to approach them , and make them leave or decide that they don't want to be hurt, which is why they avoid letting anyone into their home.

Unstable self-esteem and relationships-- pretty much, these kinds of people do not have any relationships and if they do, the relationships are not very strong and are not going to hurt this person if they end. They also have low self-esteem.

Extreme emotions that are not managed. A person suffering from Borderline personality disorders is likely to be plagued by problems with their emotions, and will be unable to manage their emotions. Imagine a child and how they manage to bounce back and forth between feelings in a matter of minutes because they don't know how to control their emotions. It's the same that happens to people with this condition.

An identity that is extremely disturbed. They aren't sure who they are, or what their mission is. They might believe they are hated by everyone, because they don't understand the way things are done.

The relationship that is in place is likely to be in chaos and most likely won't last long. Most of the time people with the disorder are not likely to be in relations that are satisfactory in any way. They might have a relationship for a brief period of time, which may be challenging and then any slight incident could trigger their emotions and they'll get off the scene in a short time. It can be difficult for people to connect with due to the difficulty with their feelings.

There are a variety of the symptoms and indicators that you should be on the lookout for when managing someone suffering from a personality disorders. It is essential to recognize the signs and symptoms to figure out whether someone is suffering from this and requires help. A few of the most severe negative side effects will be covered in the sections below.

Emotional symptoms

Let's have a examine the emotional signs of a person suffering from this type of disorder might suffer from. The people who suffer of borderline disorder those who experience more emotions than other people around them. They may experience them more for a longer time, more deeply and also more easily than others. These emotions will persist and return time and time again. You might notice that the incident that triggered them occurred a few weeks ago, however, the person is still battling emotional turmoil because it could require a long time to return to their emotional level and become stabilized once more.

The emotion can range from one extreme to the next and do not always revolve around being angry, sad or angered. People with this type of disorder can be loving optimistic, happy, and enthusiastic, however at times, these emotions can be extreme. Although they might feel these positive emotions in a way that is extreme, it doesn't mean they won't be overwhelmed by all the negative emotions around them too. In this case instead of feeling only sadness over an incident, they might experience extreme sorrow. There is a possibility of feeling humiliation and shame instead of being embarrassed by an event. The expression of anger is usually rather than anger or panic. can be seen when they feel nervous.

Most of the time, these feelings do not come unexpected. It could be that something led to the emotion initially however, since they cannot recognize and manage their emotions, their emotions are likely to get blown out of the realm of. For instance, instead simply feeling uncomfortable because you fell up the stage it will make the person believe that it's an end to the universe and everyone is laughing all the every moment. Additionally to being grieving that their favorite show has ended, they might keep this feeling of an intense sadness for the weeks to follow.

People suffering from this condition are likely to be extremely sensitive to what they see as their own lack of success and isolation, as well as criticism and rejection. This is the person for whom works with, and you're offering a suggestion to help them and not telling them that they have done any wrong. Instead of accepting it as a compliment and acknowledging that you are trying to help them, they'll get angry and believe they are being told that they been a failure and are a terrible person. The emotions will explode over the top and they could hold on to this notion for a long duration of time. The fact that they are unable to cooperate with you and believe that you're now against you will increase their feelings of loneliness because you're not going to want any contact with them.

Many times, the reason for being suicidal or injuring themselves is because the sufferer is unable to find a method of dealing with the events happening in the world around them. They don't realize that therapy, keeping things in a journal, speaking to other people, or having a healthy lifestyle would assist people deal with these emotions in a more secure and healthier manner. Because they don't know this , and their feelings seem to be all in the air They may think that these are the only options for them.

In certain cases people with this disorder will realize that their feelings are out of the norm and are not acceptable to other people however, they do not know how to manage or regulate these emotions. They decide that the most effective solution is to keep their emotions all the way. This is the exact part in which a majority of people discover the person who suffers from borderline personality disorder as the negative feelings are going to inform others about the problem and they're working to fix the issue.

There are instances when a person suffering from this type of disorder will experience a sense of joy and happiness in their lives. However, because they are more vulnerable to dysphoria-related feelings which refers to feelings of mental and emotional stress the joy might not manifest itself in the way it should. Dysphoria can cause more harm since it intensifies a lot of the problems that were already present in the individual and can make them more prominent. People who suffer from dysphoria can also experience the feeling of being victimized, feeling having no identity or feeling disorganized, causing harm to themselves or other people, and experiencing intense emotional turmoil.

If a person suffering from this condition is likely to be prone to emotional changes however, it's not the same as other people who experience mood shifts. The majority of these symptoms indicate that the individual is bouncing between being happy and experiencing sadness. However, with this type individual, this typically indicates that they will to fluctuate between anger and anxiety as well as between depression and anxiety. While the feeling of being content may occur occasionally, people will oscillate between negative emotions and anxiety.

The signs of behavior

If you are dealing with this type of disorder, it's not unusual to experience uncontrollable behavior. This can include reckless driving and spending too much money on sexual activity with multiple partners, without protection and drinking disorders, eating disorders and abuse of drugs. Additionally, the reckless behaviour can spread to other areas of individuals, like self-injury and running away and even a decision to leave jobs and relationships.

You might be wondering why someone suffering from this type of disorder has any connection to such behavior. In essence, it's a way to gain relief from the suffering they feel from their emotions. They are unable to manage their emotions they feel, and frequently they don't know the reason behind their feelings that are so overwhelming. When they indulge in this kind of behaviour, it provides them with an enjoyable sensation of relief and they begin to long for this moment of an escape from the chaotic feelings that are boiling within their bodies.

It is vital to realize that even though this can be utilized as a method to escape however, over the long run those who do this will feel more hurt due to their actions as they feel ashamed and guilty for taking part in these actions. It is a terrible cycle that is bound make someone feel worse over time. In some instances the cycle can go on until the act of impulsivity is carried out in a state of mind when a certain type of emotional pain is felt by the individual.

Self-harm

A large number of those experiencing borderline personality disorders will have problems with self-harm or with suicidal behaviors. Actually, this is among the most important factors that are used to determine whether a person really suffers from this condition or not. The management and recovery of behavior will be a challenge and a complex. There will always be the possibility of suicide throughout the existence of the person, and the probability is between 3 percent and 10 percent. Although this may not be the majority that have attempted suicide, a lot of people suffering from this condition have considered it in the past and might have tried but failed to be successful. The evidence indicates that males who are diagnosed with this disorder are nearly two times more likely than females to commit suicide after it is discovered that they have the condition. There are also speculation that a lot of men who take suicide at random may be suffering from borderline personality disorder even though they weren't diagnosed.

Even if a person isn't contemplating suicide or engaging in these kinds of thoughts, it's very likely that they will perform some form of self-injury on themselves. The motives behind the injuries vary from the motivations behind suicide in the majority of cases. The motive behind trying to hurt them without actually attempting to commit suicide is usually to keep someone from experiencing emotions, or to create normal emotions when they feel disengaged in a way of punishment or as in order to vent their anger.

When a person is trying to take their own life, they're showing the belief that people would be happier without them when the suicide has been completed. Both types of harms will be the reaction of the person experiencing these negative feelings. They believe that the abuse will help them feel normal, or make them feel better and help them feel better however it's not true.

A thing to remember is that the majority of those who suffer from this disorder aren't likely to cause physical harm to the people in their vicinity. Most of the time, this kind character disorder likely be seen in a negative light and many believe that they're a bit insane and can be a danger to the people in their vicinity. Because the majority of those suffering from this disorder were victims of problems when they were young They are extremely opposed to doing harm to others. And any damage they cause is going to be done to them and not to others.

Interpersonal Relations

The people who suffer from these kinds of disorders tend to be extremely sensitive to ways in which others are treating them. They may experience intense satisfaction and happiness when they believe that someone has treated them with great generosity. However they could feel deep sadness and anger when they sense they are being criticized by someone else or cause them to feel uncomfortable. The emotions they feel about other people will change from one day to different day, and it is contingent on how they are treated by the person or at the least the way in which they feel how they are treated. They are often concerned about losing people they trust , and don't want to feel that they're being slammed in the eyes of another person.

This phenomenon is called"black and white" thinking, or splitting and will result in the shift from idolizing other people to downgrading them. People don't realize the fact that things can be seen in different shades and only view things only in only black and white. For instance, they might be attracted to someone for a moment and then decide they don't like them or have anything to do with them. be associated with they gave them some criticism or didn't take the time to listen to them at one point.

If this type of behavior is accompanied by devaluation, idealization, and the numerous mood swings that are associated with this type of disorder, it can be very difficult for the sufferer to establish any kind of relationship, whether with coworkers, friends or family. The self-image of the individual is likely to shift from positive to negative quickly which could make it even more difficult for them to manage.

This is a huge challenge for someone affected by the disorder since they want some kind of intimacy with those who are around them. Because they are seeking intimacy but aren't getting it and tend to become focused on the patterns of attachment that they have with their partners. They are likely to feel unsecure and may shy away from others. They might also view this world to be a dangerous and dangerous one since they're unable to achieve the intimacy they seek. The problem is that they're often those who are keeping others from being around even when someone is willing to get to know them.

In certain instances of borderline personality disorder individuals may discover that manipulating is the sole method to attain the loving and intimacy they'd prefer. It's not because they wish to control those around their family, which can be found in other mental disorders. It is more about trying to convince the person to love them, and they're not sure how to go about this.

Chapter 11: What Questions Can Identify a Person with Borderline Persuasion Disorder?

Ah, yesss. What cleverly-timed method of inquiry can cause her to reveal her nefarious methods, without knowing by your secretly shady line of inquiry? Bwah hah hah. The person asking the question is sicker than BPD's.

Let's get it straight. I'm a PwBPD. I am constantly battling tons of anxiety, fear as well as the anxiety of meeting people. I have to deal with the confusion of trying to navigate through a universe that has been in my body since when I came into the world.

It is implied that we're so sinister, and manipulative to the point that, by just wearing the mental illness wizard's hat on, you can identify whether someone suffers from one of the most severe mental illnesses or is simply a jerk who is functioning normally in their limbic system, but not a single thought for the feelings of others. Because pwBPD are notoriously misdiagnosed you're seeking a skill that even that even the most experienced psychiatrists can't accomplish. How can you tell the difference between an NT who is genuinely uninterested in the swipe, or a person who has no idea how to navigate the world with toddler's processing abilities that they had been deprived of at the time that the initial'my dad was fucked by me' incident was sustained? ?

Do you be sure that with a few thoughtful inquiries you can get US believe that we know what we're doing, and expose to you the things we're not sure we're doing to keep you safe from our harm? ?

The most efficient way to do this to avoid Succubus, if that's your intention, is to concentrate on being a responsible, great stable, neurotypical. You won't need to worry about getting my shiny crow's eye.

If you were to focus on learning to be compassionate to anyone regardless of their diagnosis or perhaps just an the asshole trait, you'll discover that it's important to be willing to be open to all sorts of individuals. You might encounter a narcissist an autistic, a sociopath or a person suffering from an TBI or stroke or war veteran and discover that all of us share some of the similar traits. All of us have the capability to manipulate our thoughts using a basic self-defense strategy in which our emotions dictate to our thinking processes, and yet you can still be great individuals, along with our family, friends. Our feelings are very agitated to a screech over ridiculous dumb questions which Quora allows to be asked infinitum..

Let's think about the question this way: What do you think your reaction would be in the event that you were browsing Quora and came across the question"How can you make the Clueless Questioner admit how shallow and naive moron he truly is, by asking just a couple of questions? The person you are asking could be competent, kind, and even thoughtful to those you love however the question you asked reveals an emotional intelligence comparable to 'How can you get the hot girl at school to take notice of me and , then, be angry at her for never having noticed me previously?

It's a simple question: in the event that you were worthy of noticing...she could have done it, and manipulating someone to allow you to feel then turn the knife, is more manipulative than MY inexperienced BPD actions.

Look inside yourself and determine why you would like to find them instead of attempting to appear like normal, and properly established in your emotional intelligence, and the BPD wouldn't even be able to observe you, or would never even notice them.

For sure, if you are trying to trick an individual with BPD you're just perpetuating the violence that led us to become. That's more terrifying than anything else. Solomon, Solomon when you ask the question, show the fact that you've no care for human beings, only your own ego. Who is more sick? I'm suffering from a diagnosis and it's a very nitty one that was brought about by brutal manipulation by a few adult shamans and I've been working hard to get it fixed. If you're committed to being the most ideal person you can be to everyone around you, you don't be able to focus on the wasteful effort of seeking out those who are mentally ill.

What are the main beliefs of those suffering from Borderline Personality Disorder?

I think NT people are playing the game of fake authenticity with a certain amount in superficial charisma (a watered-down version of psychopaths) They regard other people as a possible source of manipulation, a game thing as a potential pawn in their game .

A psychopath is able to do what it wants, and an NT requires to influence (act) they possess empathy but they aren't able to take a sly swipe, to fooling one another like an online poker game.

They "think" their feelings (cognitive) they determine the most efficient method to "act" or express emotions in any given circumstance. They then modify their personalityand (outward effect) to reflect the calculated reaction

They do this naturally, and they instinctively do not consider it to be being dishonest or lying.

they keep their true feelings and thoughts inside and project outward an appropriate personality that is designed to flatter or gain the confidence of their victims/friends/families/strangers with potential

People suffering from BPD are a large personality who is dissatisfied with its own behavior and reveals a portion of themselves to other people.

inability to protect its own self when it was the most vulnerable in childhood, this can result in PTSD similar symptoms and creates BPD sufferers fear other people in a way that is instinctual

Negative reinforcement reshaped this thought in our minds (I am not good enough, I am rotten and I'm not enough and to be loved (unlovable) which is why we attempt to reveal our true selves to feel accepted as loved and not at all rotten.

People who suffer from BPD perceive others as different from what NTs and psychopaths do , but as self-image cleaners

I view people as potential judges who can either validate or deny me

The lack of positive reinforcement. NTs received. this positive reinforcement, it creates the self-image of self-love and self-confidence.

BPD individuals are constantly trying to convince themselves that they deserve unconditional love of a kind from parents. They seek to get this love out of the NTs. This is where the issues begin in interpersonal relationships.

What is it that makes those with borderline personality disorder so often drawn to relationships with Narcissists?

This is a great question, and it can turn out to be a bit complicated. However, let's back up and look at some ideas on how this might begin.

When we are talking about BPD, we are either talking about Narcissistic/Borderline types (20%) or Borderline Personality Disorderindividuals (80%) that actually are trauma survivors of childhood narcissistic abuse that appear to be borderline and meet criteria for bpd however, these types of borderlines actually grow, change, get better, and have insight and awareness. They are technically not an individual disorder. They're very different from the stereotyped BPD/Narcissists. Usually, we're talking about the 20%, the ones that change and grow.

These women also were narcissists with their mother or father throughout their the early years of their lives. Gaslighting, blame-shifting, triangulation manipulative, invalidation, or emotional abuse was all part of their daily conversations with the family member. As a young person that was all they were taught. Narcissistic emotional abuse was the way people communicated.

The second aspect is that women who suffered from childhood abuse from a narcissist later had lower self-worth low self-esteem, a lower tolerance to abuse, such as gaslighting, and felt unloved or heard, and were socially unattractive. The soul of the child was slain, so to speak.

Then , this woman gets older and chooses whom she goes to, a woman who is a narcissist. Why? This is a common dynamic that she is comfortable with, knows her surroundings, feels comfortable and doesn't consider him to be abusive, or as an person who is a narcissist. The narcissist has probably has sucked the pants off of her. He made himself appear to be all she could ever want. In her head she believes he's the exact antithesis of the narcissistic mother. But, as the narccists know that the girl is vulnerable. She has been groomed and is generous, kind but lacks boundaries and lacks self-worth. She's perfect for him so he will become the perfect match for her. Up until ....the mask begins to fall. At this point, she's already a bit in and is able to ignore the first warning sign by defending and providing him with the support he needs. She is battling with her identity, trauma worth, and the anxiety about being on her own. Additionally, she believes she's not loved, and the narcissists have convinced her that there is no one who can be as passionate about her as he is or that nobody will ever truly love her other than him.

As the abuse gets worse and the victim feels the chaos when she is bonding, like their parents used to do with her is nourished by the chaos in order to feel that you love her. She is desperate to be saved by the powerful and brutal Narcissist, and is afraid she'll never be able to live without his constant protection. In some ways she feels that she owes him what he believes is her duty. The confusion of her identity and the anxiety about being rejected makes her stuck in the current. The attraction is in such a strong way, only to fade dim within a few minutes. She is convinced that she's the only one to change , and so she remains in the fight to win him back. It's a scene that she had with her narcissistic father who didn't give them the affection she required. The cycle goes on, leading the borderline to become sometimes agitated and the narcissist calls her the victim or the crazy person. But, it's him as well as her narc family that did not see her, adored her, and nurtured her worth, and she's the insane one, while her life shared with him is truly crazy.

What are the most common behavior patterns of individuals who suffer from Borderline Personality Disorder?

It is crucial to recognize that different people have various signs of BPD Certain people are more pronounced and some with mild. It's an array.

I was first referred to the counselor by my mom as a teenager. There was no conclusive evidence at the time as the counselor was not sufficient in the small town that I lived.

My symptoms started showing after I entered college. This sequence of things is vital since it provides the answer to one of the most crucial concerns about this condition: Prior to an accurate diagnosis, you might think that you're creating a mess for everyone else and probably feel that you are a burden to your own body, but the real issue(i.e. you were hurt and abused as an infant and need to be reassured) cannot be solved. The most devastating thing that can occur to your family is that someone who had a significant role in the abuse you suffered will cause you to believe that you're good for absolutely nothing.

Traits

Chameleon effect:

My dislikes, likes behavior, personality, and usage of language could alter rapidly, and would generally be in line with my idealized persona at that moment in time.

It wasn't until after the therapy session that I realized that I did this.

2. Excessive reaction to abandonment, or perceived abandonment

I'd like to put one person in the center the universe. They then are suffocated and disengage them from me. If I sense(or feel) their distancing themselves towards me, I'll notice that my behaviour shifts towards them(all good and bad). Most often, it will result in the break-up to the friendship. I may become distant and indifferent, or act passively or they are the target of my full-on rage(more on this in the next paragraph)

3. The rage of the crowd

About 96 percent of the time I've been alive I've been convinced that I suffer from extreme anger issues.

Just yesterday, I wrote this response and stopped halfway to reflect on how, for the majority of my life I've been extremely critical of myself and believed that I'm a bad person.

I have always believed that if I were an infant, it's usually your blame. You shouldn't be sad or angry. I'm not able to recall one moment when I was praised by my parents' emotions when I was sad or sad. Not even by my teachers.

It's sad.

I was crying a lot yesterday , and I couldn't make myself write this essay.

So, we'll get back to the topic.

I realized in my sessions of therapy and reflection it was caused by a circumstance that caused the pain from the past(betrayal abandonment, shame and disrespect, for example). When I experienced any kind of anger(from mild to intense) I took a moment and tried to process every emotion, and then identify what had caused me the hurt. This is a flood of emotions that a lot of people suffering from BPD encounter. I plunge into this tizzy of emotions, and try to overcome it and calm myself.

But prior to all of this, I responded out of an impulse(more on that later) to alleviate the hurt, but ended up making it more difficult for myself and for my family and friends. This didn't help anyone. me. Zero. It's just more self-hatred over the pile of self-hatred that was already there.

4. Black and white Thinking

As I stated in the preceding paragraph the thought and your behavior is both black and white, which is good and bad, all together.

This can cause a variety of issues for those diagnosed with BPD.

Broken relationships, poorly informed choices, self-discipline not being enforced.

Nothing positive comes out of it. This was the most challenging aspect for me to master and adjust to.

5. An empty feeling and a shaky sense of self

At a time when I was totally by myself and was completely on my own and I realized that I had assumed different identities all the time without a sense of identity and it was the most frightening moment of my life. There was nothing to hold onto.

I felt as if I was in the middle of a sea with a gray skies and endless gray water. And I wasn't sure what to do to get a swimming.

I saw a glimpse into my inner psyche, and, at first, I was afraid, then apathetic I was then depressed, and finally I was numb.

6. Suicidal Idea

Yes.

This is what happens when you get up and realize that you need to be with your partner. It's a mix of'states you'd never would want for anyone else, not even for your adversaries. You're angry with yourself for having disenfranchised all those around you(point 2 3 4, 3). You blame yourself and feel sorry for yourself. You are everything bad in the eyes of you(point four). However, a tiny voice informs you that you were hurt , you put off the voice (point 5). off(point five).

7. Depression

It's true that you're feeling depressed right currently. There's so much you have to deal with and you're just trying to numb it down.

Actually, that is one of the main reasons why I chose to see a psychiatrist.

It's an endless cycle.

The therapy I received is the best thing to happen to me.

Chapter 12: What to Surmont Borderline Personality Disorder

Marginal character problem (BPD) is an issue of psychological well-being that influences the way individuals think about themselves and other people. A person with a marginal character issue might have relationships that are serious , with many high and low points and even a lot of outrageous emotions. Impatience and shifts in self-perception are also signs of a character problem that is marginal.

Someone suffering from BPD might experience mental turbulence and issues of outrage. They may also experience an anxiety about being isolated from their peers or apathetic.

Being a person with a marginal character problem is a challenge for both the person as well as their family and friends. However, it is possible to discover ways to conquer marginal character issues.

If you can find the appropriate treatment, self-improvement and methods of handling stress, you can continue living a happy and productive life even with a minor personality issues.

Chapters list

The Adaptation To Borderline Personality Disorder

5 Tips to Get the Most Value from BPD Treatment

Inhibiting BPD Without Medication

Controlling BPD and Co-Occurring Substance Abuse

The Adaptation To Borderline Personality Disorder

The process of adjusting to a character flaw is a unique experience. The patient should make an effort to find out what is working for them. It might be unique for every person however, living with a minor personality issues can be made less difficult by:

Physical activity. If you're having trouble adapting to BPD physical activity could help you regain control over your emotions and help you to balance your body. Activities such as boxing, running yoga, or cycling can be beneficial. Set aside time and effort to yourself. Although social isolation is not a good thing, taking the need to be separated from others for a period of time can provide a great opportunity to develop skills for BPD. Put aside the time to remain separate from the rest of the world and be able to focus in a way that is not influenced by other people. If you're angry or agitated with your emotions reflection can help you to reorganize your thoughts.

Writing letters or messages to people, but never writing them. It's a bit like keeping a journal, and is it is a wonderful way to work out your feelings and start to calm down. Writing down or expressing the feelings you have towards the person or situation it is possible to communicate without having your words influence your relationship. If you don't send your message you give you to reflect and revise what you wrote when the emotions that prompted it have been released. Taking breaks. In addition, removing yourself from a stressful situation will help to reduce feelings of anger and frustration.

Keeping occupied. Make a plan to keep yourself occupied with your current feelings. A small toy, such as something smooth will keep your hands busy so that your mind can focus on the specific task that must be completed.

Five Tips to Get the Most Benefits from BPD Treatment

Psychotherapy, also known as talk treatmentis an primary treatment method for a marginal character problems. The treatment of talk for BPD is focused on improving the effectiveness of your treatment as well as regulating emotions and decreasing imprudence.

Argumentative behavior treatment (DBT) is a method used to treat BPD. The mixture of individual and gathering treatment is a hallmark of DBT. Patients develop skills that are designed to aid them in managing their emotions to manage pressure and enhance connections.

There are currently no drugs that have been approved through FDA. Food and Drug Administration (FDA) specifically for BPD. The medications are even being approved to aid in the treatment of explicit indications or co-occurring issues with psychological well-being. The prescriptions for people has BPD could benefit from include antidepressants as well as state of mind stabilizers.

A medical arrangement for BPD may be the first step toward a dynamic treatment but there are a variety of techniques you can use to manage BPD:

1. Participate Actively in Your Treatment Plan

Marginal character issues require treatmentand you must attempt to be engaged, active and connected to members regardless of the treatment program. If you discover more that you will be gradually able to ask questions of a significant nature or make suggestions and communicate with the treatment providers. No treatment program is suitable for all people who suffers from BPD. It may require some effort to make it to the head.

2. Try your hand at grounding Exercises

Implementing established activities can help in figuring out ways to deal with minor character consequences. The purpose of creating practices is to help you in making your mind aware of what's happening currently. The goal is to think about the present instead of the past or what might happen in the future.

The various kinds of practices for establishing comprise:

Establishing and visual activities work out. Activities that involve sound and visuals utilize faculties to transport your mind back in time. When you are doing visual tasks, take a slow take a deep breath and look around. Take note of everything you observe. Try to notice even the smallest details. It's feasible using a sound-related activity -- take indistinguishable strides in a visual-based establishing practice but with sound. Try to notice even the tiniest sounds, and the differences between them. You'll be able to see and hear the difference creating the impression that you can perform it anywhere and people near you won't notice.

Material establishing exercises are carried out. Exercises in material establishing are ways to help you become present via the sensation of contact. Additionally, there is numerous ways to do this with enthusiasm. For example, cleaning up could be beneficial. The elastic band you wear on your wrist, and then snapping it in a delicate manner can help you get present.

The ability to tune into an app for contemplation. There are many contemplation apps that will assist in focusing your mind and help you get back to a calmer state of mind. Browse through the applications available on your smartphone or computer to determine which one is the right fit for your needs. A few moments each day with an application for guided reflection will help you stay focused.

The use of essential oils. If you feel you're experiencing dissociative experiences or symptoms of BPD Utilizing essential aromatherapy oils can help you remain conscious and calm. Find scents that include lavender or the chamomile

Breathing exercises. Learn how to inhale slowly through the nostrils and fill the lung until it is as if the lungs aren't able to absorb more air. When that happens take a breath and let circulate the lungs fully via the mouth. Then, reflect on the sensations it gives to feel the lungs expand and contract afterward.

You can research various ways of doing things until you can find what is effective for you.

3. Make an emergency Safety Plan

The most challenging elements of BPD is the intense suffering you endure. It could trigger emotional problems. There may be self-destructive thoughts or habits, for instance. If you feel observant and are in a good place create a crisis-safety plan. Plan out what you'll do in the event that you think you might cause harm to someone else or yourself.

Create a specific arrangement in case you find yourself caught in a potentially harmful situation it is likely that you won't be thinking the same way as you did when you made the agreement.

4. Get Help

In the event that you suffer from BPD it is possible that you will typically disengage from your life. The reason for this could be on the basis that you struggle with relationships or because of how you fear the judgment. It is essential to have a supportive social group of friends you can count on and trust such as your family members or friends.

You might consider joining a group for people with BPD to make connections.

5. Do self-care exercises

Health and well-being of the mind are both intrinsically connected to one the other. Being physically fit can help you in dealing with your BPD as well. Self-care is about a regular diet, exercise routine and resting enough. Find ways to relax and reduce stress that are enjoyable. Make an itinerary and schedule that includes time for things that you find charming.

Inhibiting BPD Without Medication

The possibility of overcoming BPD by prescription only is feasible but you must adhere to the guidelines and treatment program laid out by your physician or medical service provider. The drug isn't the primary treatment for BPD in the majority of cases. It's usually employed to treat specific negative effects like depression, depressive episodes or emotional attacks.

Regardless of whether you take medication to treat BPD or not, you will develop adapting capabilities and effective strategies to get through life without having chaos and its manifestations define your life.

It is essential to find methods that will work for you, and help you shift your thinking towards positive. It is also possible to be able to speak to your family and friends about your concerns. As an example, you can help your family members and friends understand how they can help you when you get angry or enthralled. Family and friends will likely have to be supportive and remain calm, but they might not know how to.

Helping someone who has Borderline Personality Disorder

Have you got a loved one or family member that's been found to be suffering from BPD? While you aren't able to force the person to seek treatment, there is ways to improve your communication and establish a solid limit and re-establish your relationship.

Young lady gripping herself

What are your thoughts about BPD

Individuals who suffer from marginal character issues (BPD) generally face significant difficulties in establishing relationships, specifically with their closest family members. Their wildly emotional experiences and tense upheavals, endless abandonment anxiety, and reckless and untruthful behavior may leave family members and friends feeling vulnerable, insecure and uncertain. Family members and friends of people suffering from BPD frequently portray their relationship as a wild and frenzied journey that lasts forever. It can be difficult to believe that you're in a position of no help when your loved one's BPD adverse effects, but they aren't when you decide to leave the relationship or the person is able to receive treatment. In any event you're in more control than you think.

You can alter your relationship by addressing your own personal responses and establishing firm boundaries of restriction, and enhancing the communication between you and your loved one. There is no magic fix, but with the right treatment and support, many people suffering from BPD can improve and their relationships can develop into reliable and rewarding. The truth is that patients who receive the best help and stability at home are likely to improve faster than those who's connections are constantly chaotic and unstable. No matter if it's your spouse, parent, child or kin, friend, or a loved one with BPD it is possible to improve the bond and your own satisfaction regardless of whether or not the person who suffers from BPD isn't ready to acknowledge the problem or seek treatments.

You can adapt everything that you can

If you find that your loved one is suffering from a character issues, be aware that the individual suffers. The destructive and dangerous actions respond to intense excruciating pain. It's true that they're not really about your wellbeing. When your beloved one behaves or says something that is afrightens you, be aware that their actions are motivated by the desire to alleviate the pain they're experiencing and is often a motive.

Understanding BPD will not necessarily resolve your issues with relationships, but it can help you know what's happening and deal with issues in more efficient ways.

Identifying the signs and side effects of BPD

Understanding the signs and effects of marginal character issues isn't always straightforward. BPD is rarely analyzed on its own and is frequently linked to co-occurring problems like, for instance, demotivation and bipolar issues or tension, a food issue, or a substance abuse. Your loved one or friend who suffers from BPD may be extremely delicate and even the smallest of things often trigger extraordinary reactions. In the event of being agitated, marginal people are often unable to be able to think clearly or silence themselves in a calm way. They can speak with frightful language or continue to behave in dangerous or unprofessional behavior. The agitation and rage can create anxiety in their relationships as well as stress for family members, companions and their companions.

A lot of people in a pleasant connection with someone suffering from BPD often discover that there is an issue that is affecting their loved one, but aren't sure about what the issue is, or if there's even a term for it. Finding out about a an issue with character that is not obvious can be seen from a place of aid and expectation.

Does your beloved one suffer from minor character flaws?

In your relationship

Do you feel that you must stomp around your beloved one, paying attention to every easily missed detail you say or perform due to a anxiety about triggering their alarms? Do you frequently hide your thoughts or feelings to avoid fighting and hurt feelings?

Do you have a loved one who moves rapidly between two boundaries (for example , quiet for a minute and then shivering the next and then suddenly depressed?) Are these emotional flashes bizarre and seeming to be absurd?

Do you have a loved one who will typically think of you as positivity or negativity, and have no middle of reference? It is probable that your character is "great," and the only person you can count on or, if they're not sure, call it "barbarous" and have never truly loved their love for them.

Do you get the feeling that you're not winning by stating that everything you say or do can be used into a weapon against you? Do you feel like your loved ones' desires appear to be constantly undergoing changing, and you're never in a position to preserve the peace?

Are you always a shortcoming? Are you constantly blamed and punished for doing things that aren't good for you? Do you feel that the person is blaming on you for actions and claims you didn't make? Do you feel that you are misinterpreted when you attempt to explain or console your partner?

Do you feel shackled by fear, guilt, or erratic behavior? Do you have a loved one who is prone to dangerous decisions, erupt into violent fury, make savage declarations, or engage in dangerous actions when they suspect that they are troubled or might quit?

If you reply "yes" to most of these questions the person you are with could have a character issue of a marginal nature.

To aid someone suffering from BPD Begin by addressing yourself

When someone close to you is a victim of a minor character flaw it is easy to get involved in courageous efforts to please and reassure the person. You could end up putting an enormous amount of your energy and effort to the person suffering from BPD in opposition to your own desires. However it's a recipe for resentment, despair or burnout and could lead to physical illness. You won't be able to assist another or make meaningful, satisfying relationships when you're exhausted and overwhelmed by stress. If you are in the event of an emergency in flight you must "put your own breathing apparatus in first."

Avoid the urge to be a part of a group. Make it a priority to maintain contact with your loved ones that help you feel better. You require the assistance of people who can listen to you out, make feel loved and give you a rude awakening whenever needed.

You're able (and authorized) to enjoy a genuine existence! You're entitled to an actual life outside of the relationship with the person suffering from BPD. It's not unheard of to block off time to relax and have an enjoyable time. If you return in your BPD relationship the two of you will benefit from your new perspective.

Join a group of care for BPD family members. Connecting with others who understand what you're going through will help. If you are unable to find an in-person group of support within your vicinity It's possible to look into enrolling in the online BPD people group.

Do not neglect your physical health. Working out, eating healthy and getting a good night's sleep can without a stretch go by the wayside when you're getting up to speed on relationship shows. Try to keep a separation from this kind of tension. When you're well-balanced and rejuvenated, you'll be more prepared to manage the pressure and control your personal emotions and habits.

Learn how to manage the tension. Being anxious or angry due to a lapse in behavior could increase your beloved one's displeasure , or even cause. Through practicing with tactile details it is possible to figure out ways to reduce anxiety while the situation unfolds and remain unaffected by the world while the weight is forming.

Marginal Personality Disorder (BPD)

If you suffer from BPD it is a time when everything seems uncertain Your connections, your temperaments behavior, thinking, and even your personality. In any event there's expectation and this guideline for signs of treatment and recovery could be helpful.

Lady in trouble holding head

What's the definition of marginal character problem (BPD)?

If you suffer from a marginal character disorder (BPD) You're likely to are feeling like you're on the edge of a rollercoaster. This is not due to the erratic feelings or connections and yet, in addition, the uncertain feeling of what your personal identity is. Your self-image as well as your goals and your choices could shift frequently in ways that seem confusing and ambiguous.

Patients suffering from BPD tend to be extremely sensitive. Many describe it as being unable to finish a nerve. Even the smallest of things can trigger exceptional reactions. When you're upset you have trouble quieting down. It's easy to see how this insecurity and lack of self-control can cause tension and unwise, even negligent behavior. When you're battling overwhelming emotions, it's difficult to be able to think clearly or remain grounded. It's possible to speak in a negative way or continue to behave in dangerous or unwise ways that cause you to feel regretful or even embarrassed a few minutes afterward. This is a vicious process that may be difficult to escape. However, it's not. There are a number of compelling BPD medicines and adapting capabilities that will help you feel feeling more relaxed and in control of your thoughts actions, emotions, and thoughts.

Chapter 13: Understanding Bipolar Better

Your doctor informs you that based upon the results of diagnostic tests, you suffer from bipolar disorder. The condition was once also known as manic depression.

The medical field defines bipolar disorder also known as manic depression as a mental disorder in which the sufferer is prone to extreme mood changes between joy and depression and the reverse. The condition can last for all of life however, there are a variety of methods to help you combat the symptoms, heal from the condition, and lead happily and productively.

To manage effectively bipolar disorder, you need to be aware

What is your diagnosis?

The reason you are suffering from the condition

What are the powers you hold to determine your situation

The most important aspect to care and treatment of the illness will be your supportive system. The support you receive from family, friends or therapist, as well as your physician is sure to help your healing. In addition, you must consider that you're the most effective weapon against the disease and decide to live a happy life regardless of it.

Diagnosis

Are you wondering how your doctor arrived at the diagnosis of your illness? This is how the diagnosis process works, simplified to your understanding.

To diagnose the condition, doctors follow the guidelines of the Diagnostic and Statistical Manual of Mental Disorders (DSM) released by the American Psychiatric Association (APA). In general to allow your doctor to identify you as suffering from bipolar disorder, the symptoms must be marked by a significant change of your mood, emotion or behaviour.

The following are the most commonly used tests to diagnose bipolar disorder:

Your doctor interviews you as well as your family member who is present during your appointment.

The determination of your diagnosis is heavily determined by the symptoms you experience as well as their duration, frequency and degree. Your physician ought to be able extract these pieces of details from both you and your family members.

In certain situations you might need to undergo lab tests to rule out the possibility of health conditions that your mood swing could be a sign. The most common are the thyroid, brain tumors and strokes.

Signs and symptoms

Because the basis of diagnosing your condition are bipolar symptoms, it is important that you know about these. Here are the symptoms and signs:

General Symptoms:

extreme mood changes that happen during episodes

Specific symptoms:

The long-lasting Elation or mania, as well as similar, but more prolonged times of sadness or feeling hopeless and sad.

A feeling of Intense irritability or on the other side the feeling of disinterest or lack of interest when it comes to everyday activities like sexual interactions.

If you are having a manic or elational episode:

It is difficult to talk quickly and have difficulty in focus. You usually switch from one topic to the next.

You are allowing distractions.

You are extremely active, participating in multiple activities at the same time.

You are prone to restlessness, and you don't easily become tired.

It's difficult to fall asleep at night.

You take dangerous risks.

You are not confident about your abilities.

You can become an impulsive.

When your depressive episode begins to set into:

It's easy to get exhausted and irritable.

You are tired or suffer from fatigue or.

It's difficult for you to make choices and concentrate your mind.

You may have memory problems.

Your routines alter, like taking a bath, eating or sleeping.

You are anxious and easily upset.

The thoughts you have are often focused about suicide attempts.

These episodes can be repeated and could last for years. In some cases they experience recurrent symptoms and others experience their normal phases in between depressive and manic episodes.

Types

The WebMD provides five (5) kinds of bipolar disorder, which are as the following:

Bipolar I is the kind of disorder in which the patient experiences the manic episodes or is experiencing severe manic symptoms that might require hospitalization or even confinement.

Bipolar II - in this kind of disorder, depressive episodes have a certain pattern. It is possible that the patient also experiences his manic episodes , but they aren't at their maximum; therefore this condition is typically classified by the term hypomania (failing to attain its full state of the mania).

Mixed Bipolar - is the type in which a person has depression and mania in the same episode.

Rapid Cycling - is the extreme form. A person is prone to experiencing many episodes of bipolar throughout the course of a year, alternating between depressive and manic. Studies show that as much as 20% of people with bipolar disorder suffer from the type of rapid cycling.

Cyclothymic Bipolar - is the kind where symptoms are not severe. The patient experiences mild depression or hypomania.

The Reasons

Treatment for bipolar or any other illness or illness is most effective when it targets the root or the underlying causes of the condition. At present medical research, we are working on figuring out the root of bipolar.

The following are the factors that could have caused you to develop your current condition:

Genetics - the genetic makeup of your body has a significant impact on the severity of your condition. Studies have proven that bipolar disorder is a genetic. It means that if anyone within your family is suffering from this disorder, you stand a higher likelihood of developing it than someone with no family background of the condition.

Brain Disorder - If there are any abnormalities in the structure and functions that your brain is experiencing, it may have caused your disorder. Through clinical studies that involve brain imaging, results reveal that the structure and function of the brains of normal individuals differ from the brains of bipolar disorder patients.

Any one of these two elements could make someone likely to be a candidate for disorder. The odds are greatest for those with both of these risk factors.

Chapter 14: The Dealing With Bipolar Disorder

There is no cure that is permanent for bipolar disorder. Once you're diagnosed with it and you are diagnosed, you will have to live to it throughout the remainder all of life. Even though you can't get rid of bipolar disorder (for at least for the moment) you can be taught to prevent it from taking over your life.

Here are some useful strategies you can employ to make bipolar disorder less overwhelming (and sometimes, minimal):

Tip No.1: Be More Active in Your Treatment

One of the most effective actions you can take to deal with the symptoms of bipolar disorder or any other illness to be precise is to know all that you can. Explore books, sites and forums on the internet that address bipolar disorders. The more you are aware of being bipolar, you'll never be astonished by anything you face; you might even discover effective methods that you might not have heard about in the absence of doing the research.

While it's nice to be aware of bipolar disorder and to share your thoughts however, you should not at any time, think that you are more knowledgeable regarding bipolar disorder than your physician. If you discover new treatment options through the internet, but do not apply these on your own. always consult your physician for his or her professional opinion to make sure that it does not hinder your progress achieved to date.

Tip No.2 Tip No.2 - Make Notes On Yourself

If you're looking to avoid your bipolar mania or depression episodes from taking over your life, you have to keep an check on yourself and watch for the smallest indication of them coming. It's usually too late to stop the mood swings from occurring when you notice the most obvious signs. Be aware of the smallest fluctuations in energy, your sleeping pattern, and the type of thoughts you're experiencing. You must catch episodes early to avoid them becoming complete manic/depressive episodes.

To organize your life You should begin making your own "mood chart" or the journal. Spend some time on your day-to-day routine to fill out your chart with details about your current emotional state and the types of things that you've thought about in recent times. A regular check of your chart can give you an idea about any changes in your behaviour that you might not be able to notice.

Tip No. 3 - Ask for help from other people

It is highly recommended (maybe even necessary) to have a solid support system when you're identified with bipolar disorders. Similar to other mental disorders, it is recommended that you have a group of people that you can confide to when you feel your illness is starting to affect you.

Family and friends The people close to you have the largest factor in whether your bipolar disorder is likely to become worse or not. Being a lone person as you don't want to burden others will only make your bipolar depression to become far more. Avoid avoiding your loved ones and your family members and instead, spend as many hours with them as you can.

Join a Support Group Sometimes talking to your close family members and friends about your bipolar disorder isn't enough. It may be a bit annoying when they don't seem to comprehend what you're experiencing. Participating in a support group will enable you to speak with others who have had similar issues and frustrations you do are, and you might get some relief by speaking with others who have had success to keep their bipolar episodes under control.

Online Groups - There's many online communities are available to join, to discuss your experiences with other people who share your experiences. The best thing about support groups on the internet is that you are able to remain completely anonymous, which is an enormous comfort for people who suffer from bipolar disorder since they're usually ashamed of their condition, even though it's not their fault. One of the groups could be joined is called the bipolar group on reddit.com. You will meet hundreds of people from all over the worldwho, as you struggle with managing their emotions.

Tip No.4 - Reduce Stress to a Minimal

Stress is among the most significant triggers of depression and manic episodes for people suffering from bipolar disorder. Therefore, you should avoid all stress you can.

Relax - Even if you suffer from a mental illness, it doesn't mean that you must be serious about it. When you go to school or the office, don't do anything that you're not able to manage. It is important to allow your brain time to recover. It will be thankful later when you succeed in doing.

Take a moment to relax each day. Even 30 minutes each day is enough to lessen the amount of anxiety your mind experiences. In the instance of a moment when you get back from school or work take a seat on a comfortable sofa, curl up with an interesting book or tune into your peaceful music, and then relax.

Sleep enough The author has mentioned numerous times in this book that sleeping lack can cause the symptoms of bipolar disorder more severe So you must ensure that you get sufficient sleep every day. Get up early and sleep each day early, but do not exercise vigorously or activities at night and refrain from drinking caffeine or alcohol since they can disrupt your normal sleep patterns.

Being a bipolar patient need not be a problem in any way. So long as you understand how to manage the condition, you will not have to be worried over the time that your bipolar disorder starts to show up and, in reality it is possible that you won't have manic or depressive symptoms for a long time, or even for a few years, and when you do, you may not notice them as often because they've been so mild.

Chapter 15: Treatments For Bipolar Disorders, Medical Treatments And Treatments for Bipolar

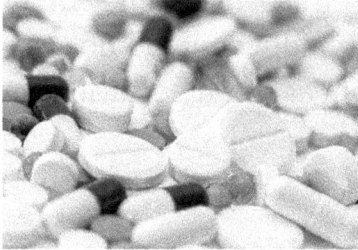

Different medications are used during the various phases of the disease, and is usually directed towards specific signs.

Mania And Hypomania

Different medications work well in treating both hypomania and mania. For instance, whether in combination with other medications it is able to treat both hypomanic and manic episodes. The main benefit for lithium lies in the fact that medication used that is used to treat the extreme episode can be utilized to treat the disorder for the longer term. It is the most effective treatment for patients with a diagnosis of bipolar disorder or those who experience an increase in hypomania or mania, along with an the sensation of euphoria or elevated mood. Other treatments that work are those that treat epilepsy, such as Valproate or Divalproex as well as carbamazepine. Atypical antipsychotics like olanzapine, risperidone and aripipra ziprasidone and clozapine and quetiapine have all proved effective in the treatment of mania as a stand-alone treatment or in conjunction together with mood stabilisers. For mild mania, just one drug could be sufficient, but when mania is serious or the episode is triggered following treatment, it is important to include another mood stabilizer.

There are a variety of factors that influence the selection of a medication but in general, these medications are equally efficient. These factors that determine the selection include the degree of a drug's previously performed, its cost for you financially when it has been approved by you on negative side effects if you suffer from another illness, and if it is efficient in treating relatives. The different medicines have distinct differences, because they can be more effective at treating certain types of mood disorders. For instance, lithium is better at treating euphoric manic episodes, and the atypical antipsychotics and valproate are both effective in treating mixed depression. People react to medication in a variety of ways however there is no method of knowing what their reaction will be. This means that you must determine what's appropriate for you, and ultimately the decision about the medication you choose to take must be based on a lengthy discussion with your physician and based from your own the experience of others.

Depression

The treatment of depression in bipolar disorder is a complex matter and antidepressants should not be only recommended as they may trigger hypomania or mania or hypomania, as well as mixed phases. The treatment for bipolar disorder depression involves the use of a mood stabilizer, when you're not taking one, or optimizing the effectiveness of your current treatment for mood stabilizers by adding another one, if you can. If, after all these steps, you still suffer from depression the doctor might prescribe an antidepressant. Antidepressants can be prescribed along with mood stabilizers in the event that you are suffering from chronic or severe depression, but with only a few manic or hypomanic symptoms or suicidal thoughts which have been reacted poorly to mood stabilizers alone. Antidepressants require some time before they begin to work.

Doctors are split and uncertain about how long antidepressants need to be maintained after they've been effective. The majority of doctors believes that the mood stabilizers ought to form the foundation of treatment for long-term. There isn't a lot of evidence to show that taking antidepressants over the long haul can prevent a return to depression, there are some who might benefit from using antidepressants in the long-term. The atypical antipsychotics , such as quetiapine, olanzapine and mood stabilizers, including lamotrigine, can be useful in treating depression.

Mixed States

In the case of mixed depression, symptoms might be more evident than manic signs, and many people are misdiagnosed as having depression. This is often a problem since mixed states respond best to standard treatment for mania, but not to treatments for depression. The way to treat multi-states is to realize that the treatment methods that are required are similar to the treatment used in mania particularly atypical antipsychotics, as well as mood stabilisers. Antidepressants can cause a mixed state more severe, even if the symptoms are mostly depressive.

The early and accurate recognition of mixed states is crucial since the most effective treatment is extremely specific and takes the time needed to work. A mix of drugs such as mood stabilizers could be the best option to treat mixed state. Atypical antipsychotics such as olanzapine are also effective in treating mixed state disorders.

Recovery times from mixed states is generally longer than recovery times for depressive or manic episodes. It is important to determine if the treatment is effective to your benefit or not. Most people feel that their treatment isn't efficient when their physician discontinue treatment or alter the treatment too fast.

The stopping of mood stabilizers could increase the severity of mixed-state symptoms. Therefore it is crucial to be patient when using mood stabilizers, as long as a few months and not stop the treatment before it has had the chance to show results.

Rapid Cycling

Being aware that you suffer with bipolar disorder caused by rapid cycling is crucial information since the treatment for it differs from the treatment for non-rapid cycling condition. For many people who experience high-speed cycling primary mood is depression. This typically does not respond well to treatment that is appropriate or adequate. Similar to mixed-events, mood stabilizers can be beneficial for those who are experiencing rapid cycling. They can also be exacerbated by antidepressants. While the response to the condition isn't as strong as in non-repeated cycling patterns, it is still of evident benefits in treating the effects of rapid cycling. Lamotrigine and valproate as well as other antipsychotics that are not typical may be beneficial. Many mood stabilizers are needed to control rapid cycling . Rapid cycling may take a number of months before it is able to settle down. If you're on the right mood stabilizers to treat the effects of rapid cycling, it's vital that you stay for long enough to allow them to be effective.

Maintenance Treatment

A lot of people suffering from bipolar disorder wish to lessen the severity of the frequency of episodes and prevent a Relapse. The repeated episodes trigger new episodes to happen more often, however the more time you're in good health is the longer you're likely to remain healthy. The key to limiting your illness is to avoid any new episodes whenever possible. Be aware that relapses are always possible , and treatment is typically long-term due to the risk that a person's body can develop the bipolar disorder. A mood stabilizer can be used to keep treatment ongoing to stop new episodes of depression, mania or mixed states from recurring. In general, lithium is considered to be the gold standard maintenance treatment, however there are other options for maintaining such as valproate, lamotrigine carbamazepine, as well as other antipsychotics that are atypical, such as quetiapine or olanzapine as well as Aripiprazole. Certain medications may be more beneficial than the other for you because each is different in its clinical properties and possible adverse consequences. It is also common for patients to need more than one medication for maintenance due to the risk of only having the partial effect of one drug.

Treatment of Anxiety

Many people suffering from bipolar disorder also suffer from severe anxiety symptoms that need to be treated along with the bipolar symptoms. Patients with high levels of anxiousness are most likely receive benzodiazepines, but it isn't clear how effective they can be in the long run.

It is important to note that benzodiazepines are addicting, and could cause additional problems, and it's recommended to discuss this issue with your physician. There are some concerns that the use of antidepressants for bipolar disorder could create rapid cycles as well as mixed state. There is no evidence to support the assertion that antidepressants can be beneficial for bipolar disorder. Most of the time, as the cause of the mood improves the anxiety will lessen. Antipsychotics that are typical in their use are beneficial for anxiety and psychotherapy is required to complement medical treatment to lessen anxiety for those with anxiety disorders.

Psychotherapy

Psychotherapy refers to a procedure which makes use of methods and strategies to improve the quality of life and overall well-being. Psychotherapy can be described in the form of "talk therapy" an expression that suggests a passive approach and does not reflect the effort necessary to resolve an issue.

Psychotherapy doesn't aim to substitute medication or serve as a treatment for bipolar disorder. However, it is certainly able to bring about positive modifications. The individual's needs and the different kinds of psychotherapy will decide the type of therapy that is required. Different kinds of therapy are employed to supplement the medications used to manage bipolar disorder. Psychotherapy's objectives are to help you remain healthy, enhance your life, and avoid or minimize the chance of relapse and the consequences.

Psychoeducation - The primary goal of psychoeducational strategies is to give information on bipolar disorder and treatment options. The majority of psychotherapy strategies for managing bipolar disorder contain some aspects of psychoeducation. These include:

Bipolar disorder is a spectrum of disorders and the course of the illness.

The role of stress and triggers and early recognition of warning symptoms.

Positive strategies for dealing with stress like a healthy life style, stress management and strategies for tackling problems.

Medication.

Cognitive and Cognitive Therapy for Behavioral Disorders CBT - Cognitive therapy (CT) and cognitive-behavioral therapy (CBT) focus on the relation between thoughts and behaviors to emotions. The primary goal of this method is to change certain habits of thought and beliefs that could affect your behavior negatively and increase the possibility of causing a worsening of your mood.

Family-Focused Therapy is a multi-faceted approach that involves the patient as well as members of their families. This method aims to improve the relationship and healthy interactions between family members and help resolve any issues that are affecting the family. Family members are part of the efforts to avoid a repeat relapse. The type of therapy is comprised of three key components: psychoeducation, problem solving and communication abilities, they are all achieved through family conversations.

Family members can benefit from psychoeducational sessions that help them to comprehend the condition and its biological cause and the impact of stressors and strategies for coping.

These sessions provide positive feedback and help to prevent communication issues that are thought of as an indication that the family members are trying to control the disorder. Family members can be seen to imitate the active listening style and are able to make positive demands.

This approach helps teach problem-solving and aid families to deal with difficulties and conflicts. As a group, the members brainstorm solutions and evaluate them, then come up with a plan for steps to take.

Family-oriented therapy has also been employed to help with suicide, by assuming that suicidal feeling is an illness. Talking openly regarding these feelings with your family members and then creating an action plan that is a group effort to avoid suicide could help you achieve some control over these worrying thoughts and emotions.

Interpersonal and Social Rhythm Therapy (IPSRT)

This is a build-up of a previous therapy known as interpersonal therapy (IPT). IPSRT emphasizes the importance of relationships between people for mental well-being. It acknowledges the role grieving and loss play when coping with bipolar disorder. It also gives patients the opportunity to speak about this and discover their own methods of adapting. Another key aspect of IPSRT when it comes to bipolar disorder is the connection to the routines of our daily life and social routines. This method focuses on how the disruption of normal social patterns can lead to an illness. There is evidence that shows regular night-day routines are essential to keep a steady mood in people with bipolar disorder. These patterns of life comprise things like when we get up and go to sleep regular routines like regular morning meetings with colleagues as well as going out to lunch. The patients who undergo this type of therapy are advised to observe their daily activities as well as their sleep/wake cycles and levels of stimulation throughout the day including the amount individuals they get in contact with. This helps them manage their daily routines so that they don't get upset.

Maintaining a Healthful Lifestyle

Many sufferers of manic depression have to make some changes in their lifestyle to remain healthy. The changes could be tiny, such as making sure to take medication or being mindful of sleeping. However certain people make major modifications like switching jobs or living a more tranquil life in a rural location. It is believed that the lifestyles of those affected by the illness can affect their stress levels and can help reduce the triggers and symptoms. There are lifestyle choices that will allow you to lead a happy life, regardless of the bipolar disorder. However, it's not advised to make major lifestyle decisions like leaving the job or ending a relationship while the symptoms are at their highest, since you might not be able to make rational decisions during those times. The best thing to do is take time to be healthy and fit and healthy, then make a decision on the things you want to do. This chapter will discuss ways to maintaining your health and enhancing your life. We'll also explore a variety of healthy habits, including exercising, healthy eating managing stress, and avoiding harmful substances.

A healthy lifestyle requires keeping a healthy balance between monitoring your health and the way you live in a way that doesn't harm your health or allow you to live your life to the fullest. There are some people who experience persistent symptoms that occur in between bipolar disorders. Depression symptoms are typically the most frequent and disrupting.

It is not necessary to constantly be occupied by the condition when you're healthy, but utilizing your medications, maintaining regularly scheduled appointments with your physician and observing your mood, triggers and warning signs will aid you in managing your illness and continue with your daily routine. You can begin implementing your plans to prevent relapses now, if you feel it is necessary.

Sleep and mood can go and go hand-in-hand. Lack of sleep or interruption to sleep could induce mood disorders; therefore an important part of your routine may include a daily routine plan that is sufficient to stimulate you and allows you maintain regular activities throughout the day to ensure you can keep your regular sleeping routines. A few everyday things such as the stress of work, jet lag and shift work could affect your sleep, and force you to make tough decisions regarding these. If your sleep routine was abruptly cut off or disrupted and you are feeling somewhat euphoric or upbeat but rather than considering it a reason to go out and do everything make sure you take it easy and reestablish your normal routines and sleeping habits. There are numerous ways to improve your life every day by engaging in meaningful actions.

Relationships

Relations aren't always fun but, when they do positive, they can be enjoyable and promote wellness. There are many ways to deal with interpersonal issues and maintain positive relations.

Your friends and family as well as colleagues and anyone you meet in your different fields of interest can all be a source of opportunity to socialize. Many people choose to use Internet chat rooms designed specifically for people with bipolar disorders or attending meetings of their local support groups because they feel accepted and respected by the groups. They also say that aside from getting help whenever they need they are also happy helping others and sharing their experience and knowledge with other members.

They can also warn people and show them that there are not all methods for managing bipolar disorder are suitable for all. It is important to note that this advice could be based on the individual's mood. The personal experience of a person is invaluable However, there are times when what individuals require is medical guidance. Keep these points in mind it is evident that other people or affected by bipolar disorder as well as their family members can be an invaluable resource. they can also help to build positive relationships. They could provide crucial services, such as employment, housing, support activities, drop-in and support programs, and advocacy.

Participating In Life

There are many activities that you can engage in such as those that ease tension or bring satisfaction, and also those that bring you a great satisfaction from as they allow you to utilize your abilities or conform to your values system. But a sole determination to achieve only can make you set unreasonable goals for yourself, and encourage you to pursue your goals in ways which is detrimental to your health. In contrast, a time of relaxation and doing nothing could make you feel unmotivated and exhausted. This is why it is important to set realistic and important goals that boosts your feelings of fulfillment without posing a risk for your wellbeing. A constant search for a goal may result in a spiral into hypomania and mania. many people feel it is beneficial to take a frequent breaks to relax. After you've engaged in an activity that is stimulating take time to relax and unwind . This will ensure you remain on the right course.

It may be beneficial to see your goals as a series of journeys rather than of one entity since this will allow you to realize that achieving your final objective is not the primary aspect, but rather each step that are taken to achieve the desired goal are the things that make your life more enjoyable. Your self-esteem could be damaged when you set unrealistic goals and recurring episodes of illness. Making realistic goals and achieving them can increase your self-esteem and feelings of satisfaction.

Setting goals with SMART objectives

The acronym SMART can assist in the setting of realistic goals. Be sure your goals are Specific, Measurable Realistic, Attainable, and time-bound.

Specific - You should set a goal that is specific so that you can know when you are successful in achieving it. For example, saying "I am trying to become fitter" isn't a concrete enough objective. Instead you could state, "I'm planning to go swimming three times per week."

Measurable - A measurable goal can help you organize your goals for what you'd like accomplish, and also to be aware of the moment you've achieved your target. E.g., "I plan to swim every week three times" can be described in other terms that are more quantifiable like "I'm going to complete 20 laps in the local pool three times per week."

Attainable - When you set goals, make sure that it's a goal that is feasible to achieve. It is possible that you will need to look for obstacles that could hinder your goals For instance the plan of swimming three times a week, twenty laps could be feasible if you did not exercise in actual time. Make sure to set a less ambitious target of 5 laps once you begin. Additionally, break down the long-term or big targets into smaller and more manageable steps. In this way it makes the long-term goal appear as overwhelming. Additionally feeling of fulfillment from all the steps. It is possible to draw the distinction between goals for short-term purposes that span from days to a week or two, mid-term goals that are achievable within a couple of months or weeks while long-term goals may take months or years to accomplish. The achievement of your short-term goals will remind you of your strengths, and long-term goals which are important to you provide you with a sense of fulfillment and meaning in your life.

Realistic Achieving a realistic goal will make you think about your real-world capabilities, and this can be a tough one. Everyone has limitations to our capabilities and goals are feasible.

To determine a realistic target it is important to consider and weigh:

Resources

Skill

Experience is required to reach the desired goal.

Consider the challenges that might be faced, including illnesses, time and current circumstances. For example, you could be offered the most glamorous job but then decide that it's the best decision for your interests to quit the job that you are currently working at. A way to judge whether a goal is worth taking on is to divide your goal into small steps and then determine the feasibility of each step. There could be a scenario that despite that a goal is important but other goals must be prioritized. Doing too many things at once is not a good idea and could be detrimental for your overall health which is why you should prioritize which goals you want to achieve within the time you have available.

Timely - Creating a timeframe to accomplish your goals will keep you focused, and remind you that there's an end point. The timeframes you set must be flexible and willing to think about other things that are happening in your life as well as any other goals that you've set. To avoid feeling pressured by deadlines, make those timeframes more flexible, and permit some extra time.

Chapter 16: How the Internet Can Do

The Internet is a very addictive medium for people today. Controlling how you use the Internet is essential, particularly for those suffering from mental illness. It is essential to establish the limits or limitations for certain information that is available.

Anyone can have access to pornographic content. Being addicted to it, as drugs, can result in the condition of bipolar or depression. It can cause depression and isolation for an individual. Being aware of it can help in reducing mental health problems.

Explore Using Different Languages

It is essential to keep your mind engaged. Watching television will only weaken your mind. Learning the language of your choice is an exercise that is mentally demanding. It could help build an improved mind through the development of concentration and focus. It can also assist a person in overcoming mental challenges.

You can leave the Car Behind

Are you able to find the school or office just a few steps from your house? If so, get rid of driving and instead walk towards the location. It is better than driving and could be a good way to exercise. It has been established that those who opt to walk instead of driving their cars are healthier and enjoy greater health benefits. Walking can also reduce stress , particularly when it comes to finances.

Be Careful of Yourself

Cleaning up and maintaining proper personal hygiene can give a person an unwavering mind and steady life. This allows him to enjoy an adequate night's sleep and more restful sleep at home.

Make sure to organize everything. It helps to have peace of mind and a calm and balanced mind. Sort out all your personal possessions and don't be afraid to ask for assistance when you need it. It can be beneficial for people who suffer from bipolar disorder.

Do some meditation

Meditation is a method to keep your mind at peace and the entire body. It allows one to ease tension, improve mental health by concentration, and cleanses it of any thoughts that may be beginning to get stuck in the brain.

Prayer Work

When someone begins to doubt themselves or lose his faith, and starts to feel as if that he's on his own and lost, all he has to do is turn around and speak to the guy who is who is there. The simple act of prayer could produce numerous miracles, therefore, make the time to practice every day. If you don't have anyone to chat with, feel at ease talking to God.

Certain studies have proven that prayer and engaging in spiritual activities are a few of the most important factors for someone to heal from the bipolar disorder. Being able to believe that one is never in isolation and understanding his motivations in life can aid in reducing anxiety and help prevent depression.

It is said that the Bible Makes a Good Companion

Instead of spending time doing something that will be a source of stress instead, why not go through the Bible instead? Keep a Bible close by and making the time to read it each day will help one feel relaxed and secure. It's a good idea to make it a routine will boost one's mood and give stability and strength.

Be a blessing to others

Are you looking for some joy and a real purpose for your life? In the event that you do, nothing is better than feeling content sharing the things someone else has done in life, and putting smiles on people's faces.

In small ways to create a bond with other people can result in the stability of your mental state. It doesn't just help individuals to feel more purposeful but also builds self-esteem. Like they always affirm, "It is better is to give rather than receive." This is true.

Miracles Don't Happen Sometimes

There's nothing wrong with thinking that things will turn out to get better, particularly when it comes to finding a cure for disease. It may bring hope to an individual, but negative results over the long term could lead to the onset of anxiety and depression. It is recommended to not to use all medical treatments that are currently not tested as they may cause more problems.

Perform a self-check-up

A diary is extremely helpful in tracking one's own progress and monitoring the possibility of Relapses. This can help and assist those going by a mental disorder such as bipolar disorder, by being aware of the signs prior to the relapse to make the appropriate adjustments. It is crucial to stay aware of the signs that are occurring before it becomes a trigger for an attack.

Patience is a Virtue that's Real

It isn't possible to achieve success and great achievements throughout the course of a single day. It takes dedication, hard work and, most importantly perseverance to get positive results, particularly in the field of health.

There isn't a quick method to treat someone suffering from a mental illness. It's a long-term objective but it is definitely achieved through perseverance, diligence and determination.

Spiritual Choices Matter

Engaging in intense religious activities is not recommended. There are many services that seem to be religious, but only emphasize emotions that could destabilize the mind of a person.

Be honest

One of the most important aspects to maintaining a healthy and stable mental health is simply by being honest. Are you not the best at this? Well, yes. It's sometimes one of the few behaviors that are difficult to master however it definitely creates positive effects on the mind. In addition, lying to others will only cause more issues so it's best to learn to be truthful.

The Cognitive-Behavioral Therapy

This type of therapy has proven to be effective to treat serious mental health disorders like bipolar disorder without medication for longer and short periods of time.

The Cognitive-behavioral Therapy can assist by altering a person's ways of thinking, behavior, and habits, and also providing the needed help. It assists in the development of strategies by experimenting with situations from real life . This helps an individual to dispel the false notions about himself.

Keep Moving Forward

The past is over and there's nothing anyone can do to alter the past. While people cannot take action however, they are able to choose to live a better life. If they're experiencing serious issues that they've had previously, they must speak to someone about it and then make a decision to move to the next step.

Despite what has occurred before, individuals can still achieve success. It's just a matter of remembering not to dwell on the past and instead utilize it to create the best of tomorrow.

Reach the Correct Goals

Do you want to start an entrepreneurial small-scale company? Do you dream of becoming a corporate manager? You can write some goals for your life so you can as long as they're achievable. The life goals can be a source of inspiration to people to look forward towards and achieve them. Setting goals that appear to be complicated can bring one down It is better to be realistic about the process.

The Neurofeedback Treatment

The Neurofeedback is one of the most effective strategies in the treatment of bipolar disorder. It aids in recovery by enhancing the mind and enhancing self-control and concentration. Professionals offer the necessary help for people suffering from a mental disorders, however, this treatment can be expensive.

Combining these treatments with cognitive-behavioral therapy as well as some adjustments to lifestyle can be very effective. Neurofeedback is a proven treatment in the field of mental health.

Don't be worried about the money

The thought of financial issues whether someone owes money or is unable to pay for something, can cause a person to be upset and cause him to feel depressed. It is important to manage the finances well or at the very least seek help from friends or family members whom one can trust. The habit of overspending is a common problem for those with bipolar disorder, so managing the credit cards properly can help improve your mood.

Conclusion

Disorders of the mind like bipolar can be very debilitating particularly when patients don't receive the assistance they require from their family and friends. Uncertainty about their condition can restrict them and increase their mood swings and depression.

Bipolar condition isn't a normality. It is a psychological disorder typically caused by several circumstances. It is usually an ongoing struggle but bipolar patients are able to be treated with the use of psychotherapy and medications for psychiatric issues, particularly when they are treated as frequently as is possible.

You or someone you care about suffers from manic depression I hope that this book was helpful in helping you comprehend this condition more clearly. Always remember that there's hope for complete recovery and treatment, or at a minimum to reduce the frequency of the episodes and manageable for those suffering from the condition.

If it's an occasional condition of bipolar disorder, or a severe one it is always suggested to consult an experienced medical professional who is skilled in psychiatric issues. Do not put your life in the hands of chance as you may cause worse harm than benefit if you attempt to self-medicate in order to combat a serious psychiatric condition such as manic depressive.

If you've completed reading this book, ensure you take the appropriate steps to ensure that bipolar sufferers receive the appropriate medical treatment and the complete compassion and support of family members and friends. Don't let the condition become more severe before taking actions. When you decide that the problem serious enough to warrant being taken care of, it could be too to be too late for you or someone you love dearly.